THE SUMMER BOOK

"Won't you come into my garden? I would like my roses to see you." ♥ Richard Sheridan

SIGN YOUR NAME

Here Comes Summer...

"The easeful days,
   the dreamless nights;
The homely round of
   plain delights;
The calm,
   unambitioned mind,

The simple stuff
of summer time."

After Austin Dobson ♡

THE SUMMER BOOK
from the
HEART of the HOME

by
Susan Branch

Little, Brown and Company
Boston · New York · Toronto · London

FOURTH PRINTING

ISBN 0-316-10666-6

"The Sun and Fog contested" by Emily Dickinson from The Poems of Emily Dickinson, Thomas H. Johnson, ed. Copyright © 1951, 1955, 1979, 1983 by the President and Fellows of Harvard College. Reprinted by permission of The Belknap Press of Harvard University Press and the Trustees of Amherst College.

Excerpt from "On the Sunny Side of the Street," lyrics by Dorothy Fields and music by Jimmy McHugh. Copyright © 1930 by Shapiro, Bernstein & Co., Inc., copyright renewed. Used by permission of Shapiro, Bernstein & Co., Inc., Hal Leonard Corporation, and Aldi Music and Irene Adele Publishing Co., care of the Songwriters' Guild of America.

"Everything Grows in My Mother's Garden" from On Flowers. Copyright © 1992 by Kathryn Kleinman and Sara Slavin. Used by permission of Chronicle Books.

Excerpt from "A Summer Song" by Clive Metcalfe, Keith Nobel, and David Stuart. Copyright © 1964, renewed and assigned to EMI UNART CATALOG INC. Used by permission of Warner Bros. Publications, Inc.

RRD-IN
Published simultaneously in Canada by Little, Brown & Company (Canada) Limited

PRINTED IN THE UNITED STATES OF AMERICA

My Grandma's memories are now my memories too, they are a part of me like she is. For all the summers of her childhood, beginning when she was born in 1909, she traveled with her mother & dad & 7 sisters & brothers in their white, open-air "touring car" (like in Cheaper by the Dozen) from their 3-story home in Sioux City, Iowa, to their "camp" on McCook Lake on the South Dakota border. The cottage had no electricity but it had a huge screened-in sleeping porch where the family slept under the stars. They all helped in the garden; the saying went "We eat what we can & what we can't, we can!"

She was free as a bird, could run like the wind & swim like a fish; her dad nicknamed her "Spitfire," & her carefree summers there are a sublime memory in her life where hardly anything ever happened at all— one perfect day onto another.

This book is dedicated to her & to our memories of all the summers gone by & the ones still to come. And to your memories, too — make some this summer — it will never come again.

TABLE OF CONTENTS

" 'Just living is not enough,' said the butterfly.

" One must have sunshine, freedom,
and a little flower.' "
♥ Hans Christian Andersen

A LITTLE SEASON OF LOVE & LAUGHTER

The Summer Garden

" I meant to do my work today —
But a brown bird sang in the apple tree,
And a butterfly flitted across the field,
And all the leaves were calling me."
♥ Richard Le Gallienne

Outside the kitchen door: we dug a rectangle in the middle of the lawn — 12' x 24' (not too big!).

Then Joe built a fence around it and painted it white.

He made paths and raised beds.

It has a garden gate. ♥

Upon which I hung my hat.

Inside there are fresh herbs & vegetables & outside there is a flower border of (mostly) annuals.

for my KITCHEN GARDEN

CLEOME

TOMATOES!   MARIGOLDS!   TOMATOES!

LEMON CUCUMBERS

Gladious, Lilies,

HERBS

POTATOES

WATERMELON

PEPPERS

ONIONS

LETTUCE

Dahlia PomPoms, Cleome

CLEOME

HERBS

LETTUCE   RADISHES

Iceland Poppies, Baby's Breath, Cosmos,

Snapdragons, Petunias, Sweetpeas,

It's small enough so I can take care of it myself. The flowers & the fence hide the ever-changing mess inside. ♥♥ I put different things in every year — like redecorating, only with flowers! ♥

10

A Garden of Herbs

They are steeped in superstitions & folklore — witches, fairies & countrywomen have used them to cure everything from heartache to gout. They are symbols of such virtues as courage, friendship, fidelity & remembrance. They can be grown casually, here & there in the garden; they also make beautiful formal gardens, particularly in the old-fashioned knot garden. You'll find them growing wild in the woods, in cracks & crevices of rock walls, on old paths to the sea & in pots on balconies & window sills. Many herbs are perennial & return year after year. There are famous herb gardens all over the world which are visited regularly by people like me who adore the history, fragrance, color, delicacy & charm of the herb garden. They're easy to grow & a fresh, natural way to flavor foods — no kitchen garden would be complete without them. ♥

POTTED SUMMER

BASIL   ROSEMARY   PARSLEY

LIFE'S LITTLE NECESSITIES

Favorite Herbs
easy to grow
good for | you too

PARSLEY

BASIL is the symbol of love & devotion; an annual that grows best in full sun — pinch flowers off as soon as you see them. Basil is fragrant & delicious with tomatoes, cheese, pasta, salads & eggs. I grow lots of it so I can make & freeze pesto for the winter. ♥

ROSEMARY For remembrance. Rosemary likes sun & is a tender perennial so it must be taken inside in winter where temps. fall below zero. Great with lamb, pork & chicken, with roasted potatoes, in pasta salads, baked with goat cheese — on tomatoes, focaccia, & in salad dressings — brush rosemary butter on grilled fish ♥

MINT For virtue. Spearmint & peppermint are most popular but others, such as apple, orange & pineapple mint, are lovely too. Mint likes partial shade; it's a hardy perennial that can take over a garden, so it's best kept in a pot. Fresh mint adds a cool, refreshing flavor to many foods. It's great for garnishing fruit salads & iced drinks — famous in mint juleps. Classic with lamb, minced into peas, & in tabbouli. ♥

CHIVES A perennial requiring full sun or part shade. Pull the flowers out by bottom of tough stem before they go to seed. Delicate flavor, wonderful in cream cheese, any potato dish, with peas, eggs; in salads, with fish & on sandwiches. Tie little bundles with chive leaves. ♥

ORGANIC VITALITY

FRENCH TARRAGON
Another perennial but it needs protection from frost — cover it with leaves; it prefers sun but not too hot or humid. It's most important to get French Tarragon & not the less flavorful Russian variety. It is delicious in vinaigrette & a must in bearnaise sauce — wonderful over buttered new potatoes. Use it for chicken, in mayonnaise for cold salmon & salads. ♥

THYME
The herb of courage, thyme is a hardy perennial that loves full sun & fairly dry soil. Bees love thyme. A little goes a long way in many dishes: fish & seafood salads & chowders, onions, stuffings, salads & vegetables. Makes delicious herb butter for steaks or chops or on pasta.

CILANTRO
An annual that goes to seed easily in too-hot weather — reseeds itself & with a little mulching it will even grow in the snow. The fresh leaves are called cilantro but the seeds are called coriander & taste very different. Cilantro is great with tomatoes — perfect in all Mexican food — salsa, in ceviche (cold scallop & lime salad), & on quesadillas. Its great in chili & curry, with cheese & in salads. ♥

DILL
is a hardy annual; plant in sun & pinch off flowers as soon as you see them. Tall & graceful, this lacy herb is disliked by witches (in case you're having a problem☺), but best on poached fresh fish like salmon, on cucumbers, in potato salad & cream cheese dips, in vegetable salads & omelets. ♥

OTHER NOTABLE GROWABLES
For the herb garden

NASTURTIUM

Flowers taste like radishes — they come in peach, yellow, orange — beautiful in salads, leaves too. Easy to grow in full sun.

BORAGE

Sweet-tasting blue flowers — float them in summer drinks, cold soups, salads, whipped cream.

Summer Savory
Lovage
Oregano
Salad Burnet
Sage
Lavender
Marjoram

Roman Chamomile

Boil flowers for steam facials. Make tea for relaxation. Plant around garden bench.

LEMON VERBENA

A shrub that can get to 6' — plant it near a window to bring fragrance inside; in bath; scented bunches; garnish lemonade.

HERB NOTES

Grow herbs near your kitchen door for easy access. Start small. A small garden is no trouble but still gives joy. Chop, tear, crush herbs to release flavor. Buy the biggest, healthiest plants at your nursery. The perennials will come back year after year. If you live in snow country, cover them with leaves — some of them will thrive even in mid-winter — a treat! Use 3 times as much fresh herb as dried — if a recipe calls for 1 tsp. dried, use 3 tsp. fresh. Plant garlic cloves near roses to promote health & growth. When a plant is small, pinch off top leaves — it will branch out & get bushier, good for basil.

Crush & throw a couple of handfuls of cooling mint into your bath — you can make a muslin bag to fill with herbs & hang under the running water. Choose lavender, sage, rose petals, chamomile, lemon verbena (nice with lemon peel in it). Oatmeal softens water — mix it with herbs. Pick herbs first thing in the morning. Pick whole stems of chives & parsley starting from the outside near base of plant. Plant Roman chamomile or low, spreading thyme under garden bench or picnic table. When you step there fragrance will be released.

P L E A S U R E S & V I R T U E S

NERVES. 'BURNED OUT' BLOOD? NO PROBLEM — MIX HONEY WITH INFUSED SASSAFRAS BARK

HONEY FOR TEA SOOTHES NERVES. ♥ HONEY TO TASTE. ♥

& VOILÀ! YOU'RE CURED. ♥ BEE KISSES ♥ WARM 2 C. HONEY & MIX IT WITH 7 SPRIGS OF THYME. SPREAD ON BISCUITS.

FLOWER NECTAR FOR WAFFLES & CORN BREAD, MIX SOFTENED BUTTER WITH HONEY TO TASTE. ♥

" Prone to revenge,
the bees,

a wrathful race..."

Samuel Bagster

...but, oh! Honey!

FLU? JUICE OF 1 LEMON, SHOT OF WHISKEY, SPOON OF HONEY INTO HOT WATER. GOODNIGHT.

A KNOT GARDEN

KNOTS ARE FORMED BY CONFIGURATIONS OF DIFFERENT HERBS SHAPED INTO SMALL COMPACT HEDGES THAT OVERLAP. THIS IS A SIMPLE DESIGN AND EASY TO DO. YOU'LL FIND NICE DESIGN IDEAS IN BOOKS ABOUT HERBS.

ALL 3 HERBS USED IN THIS KNOT GARDEN NEED FULL SUN & ALL ARE ESPECIALLY HARDY. THEY ARE EASY TO CLIP INTO COMPACT LITTLE HEDGES; THEY ARE AROMATIC & THEY ALL FLOWER. ♥ USE SQUARED PAPER AND STRING TO HELP DESIGN YOUR LITTLE KNOT GARDEN.

GERMANDER: TEUCRIUM CHAMAEDRYS, LIBIATAE. 16" CUT ON ANGLE FOR STRENGTH
LAVENDER: LAVENDULA SPICA, DWARF HIDCOTE. 18" CLIP LIGHTLY AFTER FLOWERING
SANTOLINA: CORSICA, COMPACT DWARF VARIETY. CLIP IN SPRING TO BOX SHAPE

17

Fragrant Flowers

Roses
Jasmine
Stock
Lily of the Valley
Peony
Wisteria
Nicotiana

Lavender

EARTH LOVES a garden of fragrance

FOR PEACE of mind and a TRANQUIL SPIRIT

Sweet Pea
Mock Orange
Carnation
Freesia
Lilac
Snapdragon
Lily
Honeysuckle

PLANT A LOVELY CUTTING GARDEN — ♥ ♥ BRING FLOWERS INDOORS.

Everything grows in my mother's garden:
      camellias, delicate pinks & whites, splendid scarlets,
graceful lilies, regal iris, cheerful ranunculus.
      Good things to eat grow in my mother's garden.
Tomatoes as sweet as fruit, peppers red & green,
carrots, sugar peas, baby lettuce.
      'Coleslaw grows in my Nena's garden.'
That's what my son brags to his friends.
A city child, he thinks magic transforms garden treats
      into his favorite dish.
      It is magic, I tell him, Nena's magic.
Her grace with all things green & growing. There
      must be special secrets in my mother's garden.
      All of us, family & friends, we marvel at my
mother's garden. She must know secrets, we think.
      And, she does — secrets of generosity, kindness,
compassion, of life lived honestly, imaginatively, well.
      Still trim in gardening clothes,
she brushes dirt & leaves from her hands
and comes to greet us.
      There's much I wish I learned from my mother:
French seams, southern chicken, patience, painting,
some medicine. For these things I have no aptitude.
      But now, a mother myself, I crave a secret or two.
I want to garden, as she does with grace & love & skill.
      We ordered bulbs together this summer. She claims
to envy me my tulips. And I? I want only this,
my son to say one day:
      Everything grows in my mother's garden."

HELPFUL
HOUSEHOLD HINTS

Hang cheesecloth bags of yarrow, mint & lavender in your closets & cupboards to repel moths & sweeten the air. ♥

Bay leaves & whole cloves keep ants & pests out of cupboards — and ants won't cross a chalk line (making the pitcher's mound a perfect picnic place).

Feed birds all winter & they will reward you by sticking around & stuffing themselves with your insects all summer. ♥

You can buy ladybugs in garden stores & set them free in your garden — they eat garden pests & feast especially upon aphids. (They are also good luck, like hummingbirds.)

For bee & wasp stings — you can rub on summer savory or run for an ice pack, hold it on the spot while you make a little paste from baking soda & water. ♥

Light citronella "bug bucket" candles 1 hour before your backyard party. If you invite me to your party you won't need insect repellent because they'll have their favorite food & you will be safe. Otherwise Avon Skin So Soft works great & amazingly doesn't smell too bad; Skintastic is good too. ♥

Drag your fingernails over a bar of soap before you work in the garden. ♥ (Keeps dirt out.)

Put a saucer of beer in the garden — snails & slugs LOVE beer & will commit suicide by drowning in it. ♥

"SOME PEOPLE LIKE TO MAKE A LITTLE GARDEN OUT OF LIFE & WALK DOWN A PATH." ♥ JEAN ANOUILH

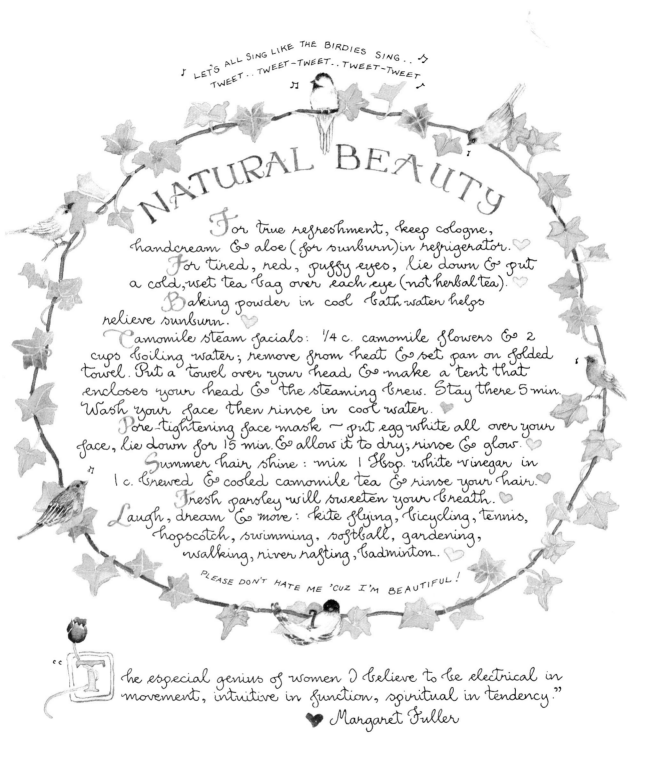

NATURAL BEAUTY

For true refreshment, keep cologne, handcream & aloe (for sunburn) in refrigerator. ♡

For tired, red, puffy eyes, lie down & put a cold, wet tea bag over each eye (not herbal tea). ♡

Baking powder in cool bath water helps relieve sunburn. ♡

Camomile steam facials: ¼ c. camomile flowers & 2 cups boiling water; remove from heat & set pan on folded towel. Put a towel over your head & make a tent that encloses your head & the steaming brew. Stay there 5 min. Wash your face then rinse in cool water. ♡

Pore-tightening face mask ~ put egg white all over your face, lie down for 15 min. & allow it to dry; rinse & glow. ♡

Summer hair shine: mix 1 Tbsp. white vinegar in 1 c. brewed & cooled camomile tea & rinse your hair. ♡

Fresh parsley will sweeten your breath. ♡

Laugh, dream & move: kite flying, bicycling, tennis, hopscotch, swimming, softball, gardening, walking, river rafting, badminton. ♡

PLEASE DON'T HATE ME 'CUZ I'M BEAUTIFUL!

"The especial genius of women I believe to be electrical in movement, intuitive in function, spiritual in tendency."
♥ Margaret Fuller

TO KEEP CUT FLOWERS
FRESH — REMOVE ALL
LEAVES, STEMS & THORNS THAT
GO UNDER WATER.

THE LIGHT TOUCH

CLEAN YOUR WINDOWS FOR MORE LIGHT ~ REMOVE HEAVY CURTAINS & HANG SOMETHING THIN & FLUTTERY.

COLLECT LACE DRESSER SCARVES OR SHAWLS; DRAPE OR PIN THEM TO THE TOP OF CURTAINLESS WINDOWS.

SET OUT BOWLS OF PEACHES & TANGERINES OR BASKETS OF SHINY YELLOW LEMONS, LOTS OF FRESH FLOWERS.

LIGHTEN COLORS IN YOUR ROOMS. REMOVE HEAVY QUILTS & SPREADS ~ USE OLD-FASHIONED WHITE COTTON (BLEACHABLE) BEDSPREADS. REPLACE COUCH PILLOWS WITH LIGHTER COLORS; TAKE UP RUGS. SUMMERIZE!

OLD FLOWERED CREAMERS MAKE NICE VASES FOR WILDFLOWERS ~ FIND THEM IN YARD SALES.

SEASHELLS & BIRD HOUSES MAKE WONDERFUL SUMMER MOTIFS.

TUCK A BOUQUET OF DRIED FLOWERS AMONG THE LOGS IN YOUR FIREPLACE.

REMOVE ALL THE COATS, HATS & SCARVES FROM THEIR HOOKS & REPLACE THEM WITH STRAW HATS, & A GARDEN SMOCK.

HOME SWEET HOME

GROW SOMETHING SWEET SMELLING NEXT TO YOUR DOOR, LIKE HONEYSUCKLE.

FLOWERS ON EVERYTHING ~ QUILTS, NEEDLEPOINT PILLOWS, LINENS, PRINTS & PAINTINGS, CHINA CUPS & BOWLS, RUGS, WALLPAPER ~ IN POTS & VASES.

A PALETTE OF COLOR TAKEN FROM ENGLISH CHINA ~ PINK & PALE GREENS, LIGHT BLUE, WHITE & PEACH, COOL, LIGHT & AIRY.

COLLECT ALL THE WEDDING PICTURES OF YOUR FRIENDS & FAMILY (PAST & PRESENT), FRAME & DISPLAY THEM IN JUNE. ♥ HAVE A LOVE-LY SUMMER. ♥

IMAGES OF SUMMER

Clothes drying on a line

Fireflies
TWINKLE
in the dark

Books
to read

wild blueberries

Foghorns
&
lighthouses

Lobsters on the
Beach at Sunset
SWIM TO REMOVE
BUTTER DRIPS

Saturday
Morning
Farmers'
Market

Roses on a Pickett Fence

Cucumber
Sandwiches

SWIMMING IN THE
OCEAN ON HOT NIGHTS

Beach
Umbrellas

yard
Games

Summer Nights
dark warm
downtown quiet
& Window shop
eat ice cream

"What is life? It is the flash
of a firefly in the night. It
is the breath of a buffalo in the
wintertime. It is the little shadow which runs across the grass
and loses itself in the sunset."
♥ Crowfoot

Appetizers and Sandwiches

25

APPETIZER IDEAS

Marinate chunks of swordfish in soy sauce for about an hour — wrap pieces in bacon, hook with water-soaked toothpicks & grill. ♡

Quick Pizza Hors d'oeuvres: Brush a large Boboli bread with olive oil, sprinkle over minced garlic & grated mozzarella; lightly sprinkle on red pepper flakes, then some chopped fresh basil, & then thin slices of fresh tomato. Sprinkle with Parmesan & bake in a preheated 475° oven for about 12 min. With a pizza wheel cut into small bite-sized squares. ♥

Sweet, ice-cold Littleneck clams on the half-shell with lemons & cocktail sauce is a staple at backyard parties on the Vineyard. ♡

A plate of cucumber sandwiches goes just swimmingly with icy Pimms Cups (p. 119) on croquet day. Egg salad is good, too! (See p. 42 for other sandwich ideas.) ♥

Bowls of fresh sweet cherries, strawberries — or iced radishes — all perfect and in season.

Don't forget these summer appetizers — you'll find the recipes in my other books: Stuffed eggs Clams Casino, Grilled Peppers, Flowers & Cheese, Fried Squid (i.e. Calamari), Smoked Bluefish Paté, & Stuffed 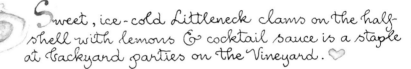 Nasturtiums. ♥

"Oh come let us play a game of croquet,
Cried rosy-cheeked May to her sister one day.
They played a great game, and then had another;
May won the first, but Jane won the other."
♥ Virginia Gerson

TWO
STUFFED MUSHROOMS

These are a nice combo, VERY easy to do — make them ahead & pop them in the oven when your guests arrive & there you are! ♥

Boursin

30~40 med. mushrooms
1 c. Boursin cheese
3 tbsp. butter, melted

Preheat oven to 350°. Wipe mushrooms with damp towel — remove & discard stems. Brush the bottom of each mushroom with melted butter & fill cavity with cheese. Place them on an ungreased cookie sheet, bake 30 min. ♥

Sausage

40~50 med. mushrooms
1 lb. pork sausage
1 tbsp. honey
1 tsp. whole leaf sage, crumbled

½ tsp. thyme
¼ tsp. allspice
pinch cayenne
Parmesan

Preheat oven to 350°. Wipe mushrooms with damp towel — remove & discard stems. Combine all ingredients except Parmesan & mound mixture into mushroom cavity. Sprinkle with just a bit of Parmesan, place on ungreased cookie sheet, bake 30 min. ♥

"When I was a little kid, of course, I was brown all summer. That's because I was free as a bird — nothing to do but catch bugs all day —" Roy Blount, Jr.

SEA BREEZES

An elegant hors d'oeuvre.

endive	pickled ginger
cream cheese, softened	fresh lime juice
smoked salmon	fresh dill or parsley (opt.)

Separate endive stalks, wash & dry thoroughly. Spread wide end of each stalk with about a tablespoon of cream cheese. Put a thin slice of smoked salmon on top & top that with a piece of pickled ginger. Arrange them on a nice platter & squeeze lime juice over all. Decorate with tiny sprigs of dill or parsley if you like. ♥

Grilled Cherrystone Clams

Cozy~ eat them right off the grill with little forks. You need a covered grill for this.

First you have to go out & dig 2 or 3 dozen hard-shell clams (OK, you can get them from your fish market, or mine, p. 84). Rinse them off & set them, tightly packed, tops up (poor babies) on a very hot grill. Cover the grill with lid & cook 10 min. or so, till they open. Discard any that don't open. Squeeze lemon juice over all. While they are cooking, melt butter & minced garlic in a small pan on top of grill. Remove meat from shells, dip & eat. Also delicious with fresh tomato salsa. ♥

" . . . Bread and butter, devoid of charm in the drawing-room, is ambrosia eaten under a tree."
♥ Elizabeth von Antrim

TORTILLA ROLL~UPS

Makes 40 pieces

These look wonderful served in a large shallow basket ~ they're healthy & good. Take them to a 4th of July picnic. ♥

8 large flour tortillas
2 c. (16 oz.) hummus (or Boursin cheese)
1 c. watercress leaves or radish sprouts

2 c. grated carrot
1 c. thinly sliced red onion
1 c. thinly sliced yellow pepper
salt & pepper, to taste
40 short (6") wooden skewers (opt.)

Lay out tortillas. Spread hummus thinly over entire tortilla, right up to the edge. Sprinkle other ingredients evenly over the tortillas. Roll up as tightly as possible, using a bit of additional hummus to seal edges, if necessary — press gently to "glue" it all together. Use a serrated knife to cut off & discard uneven ends, & cut the rest into 1 3/4" pieces. The skewers make them look good: pierce each piece, arrange on tray & serve.

OUR LITTLE V-DUB, DRESSED & READY TO GO TO THE TOWN PICNIC. ♥

SNAKE BITES

Serves 4~8

8 large Anaheim peppers
8 sm. peeled & cooked shrimp
8 thin slices jack cheese
    (about 3 oz.)
½ c. flour
2 eggs, beaten
vegetable oil for frying

Jalapeño mayo

½ to 1 whole jalapeño pepper,
    seeded & chopped
½ c. mayonnaise
1 tbsp. fresh lime juice
2 tsp. cilantro, roughly chopped

Make the Jalapeño Mayo: seed the pepper, chop it & put ½, with mayonnaise & lime juice, into food processor. Process well —taste— if it's not hot enough, add more jalapeño. Stir in cilantro & chill. Turn broiler to highest setting. Put peppers on a broiling pan & as close to heat source as possible — leave oven door ajar. Watch carefully; blacken all sides, turning with tongs. Remove; when cool, peel them, split them length-wise (carefully) & remove seeds. Stuff peppers with cheese & shrimp (don't overstuff, edges should meet). Heat 1" oil in skillet. Dip peppers in eggs, roll in flour & fry, split-side facing downward first. Turn when browned (about 30 seconds) & finish other side. Remove, drain on paper towels. Serve with Jalapeño Mayo. ♥

"There is more to life
than increasing its speed."
♥ Gandhi

BOWL OF VEGETABLES

Gather at the picnic table & set out a big wooden bowl of grilled & roasted garden vegetables — gorgeous color, wonderful flavor. Have a hot, crusty loaf of peasant bread, or serve Crostini (p. 34) alongside. ♥

Include in your bowl:
    Rosemary Potatoes ⎫
    Green Beans   ⎪
    Carrots   ⎬ see pgs. 74 & 75
    Red Peppers   ⎪
    Garlic   ⎭
    Plum (Roma) Tomatoes ~ bake in 400° oven,
        or cook on grill till soft.
    Onions, sliced or whole, brush with olive
        oil, bake at 500° till brown.
    Portobello Mushrooms (p. 57)
Sprinkle over Niçoise or Calamata olives, garnish with sprigs of rosemary or fresh basil leaves. Serve warm or at room temp. Drizzle lightly with Roasted Veggie Dressing:

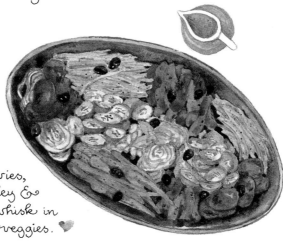

1/4 c. balsamic vinegar
2 anchovies, mashed
1 tbsp. Dijon mustard
1 clove garlic, crushed
1 tbsp. parsley, minced
1 tbsp. fresh rosemary leaves
1/2 c. olive oil

Whisk together vinegar, anchovies, & mustard; add garlic, parsley & rosemary. In a thin stream, whisk in olive oil. Drizzle over roasted veggies. ♥

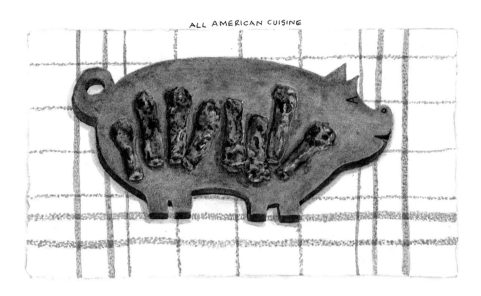

COCKTAIL RIBLETS

Serves 8

3 lb. Chinese-style pork ribs
1½ c. pineapple juice
1 c. soy sauce

¼ c. + 2 Tbsp. brown sugar
¼ c. + 2 Tbsp. Worcestershire
1 Tbsp. dry mustard
3/4 tsp. Tabasco

Cut ribs into individual pieces; drop into boiling water, cook 10 min., drain. Combine all other ingredients. In a large bowl, pour sauce over ribs & mix well. With tongs, transfer ribs to med. hot grill; cook 15-20 min., basting often. 💗

CHICKEN WINGLETS

24 pieces chicken winglets
½ c. honey
⅓ c. soy sauce

2 Tbsp. Dijon mustard
½ tsp. red pepper flakes
1 tsp. minced ginger root

Preheat oven to 325°. Wash chicken & dry; place pieces into a shallow baking dish. Mix together remaining ingredients, pour over winglets. Bake 1 hr. Cool. Serve warm. 💗

"We had mighty good weather as a general thing, & nothing ever happened to us at all." Mark Twain

oe remembers Bart from his childhood summers spent on the Vineyard. Her real name was Ruth Gardner but somewhere along the line she was given the name Bart because, her children said, she looked like a Bartlett pear. ♡ When I met her she was 92 years old & bustling around her kitchen surrounded with holiday-making grandchildren, & great grandchildren too. When I asked her for this recipe, she rattled it off from memory using the mantra "one-eighth, one-quarter, one-half, one cup." Beloved Bart is gone now, but not forgotten. So, here is a Gardner Family tradition:

Bart's Cocktail Cheese Biscuits
350°

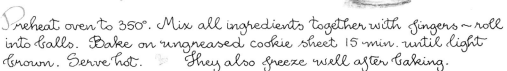

1/8 tsp. salt
1/4 lb. butter, softened
1/2 lb. sharp cheddar, grated
1 c. flour
dash of tabasco

Preheat oven to 350°. Mix all ingredients together with fingers ~ roll into balls. Bake on ungreased cookie sheet 15 min. until light brown. Serve hot. ♥ They also freeze well after baking.

"Walled round with rocks as an inland island,
The ghost of a garden fronts the sea."
♥ Algernon Charles Swinburne

Fettuntas

CROSTINI

Bruschetta

Glossary: Crostini are thin slices of French bread which have been crisped under the broiler or on the grill. Fettuntas are crostini which are rubbed with garlic & brushed with olive oil before crisping. Both make wonderful bases for cheese spreads & dips, etc. Bruschetta are the crisps topped with the fresh tomato mixture below.

These are so delicious they are worth making a meal around. We had a wonderful all-girl Summer B'day Lunch ~ the menu: fresh garden gazpacho with lobster chunks, rosemary & orzo pasta salad with Niçoise olives, & these mouth-watering bruschetta & crostini ~ 3 kinds. For dessert we had a plate of fresh summer fruits, a big lemon-filled Coconut Birthday Cake (p.108) & Homemade Fresh Strawberry Ice Cream (p.103). Everything easy & make-ahead. My fave. ♡

First make the crostini or fettuntas. Cut a French bread baguette into 1/3" slices ~ either broil until crisp, or rub the bread with a cut piece of garlic, brush with olive oil & then broil or grill until crisp. Choose from toppings or serve plain with a dip. ♡

BRUSCHETTA

You can spread crostini with soft goat cheese, then broil, then pile on the tomato mixture ~ experiment! ♡

1 c. fresh summer tomatoes, minced & drained	1 Tbsp. olive oil
2 Tbsp. fresh basil, slivered	a splash of balsamic vinegar
2 Tbsp. green onion, minced	pinch of red pepper flakes (opt.)
1 clove garlic, minced	salt & pepper
	whole basil leaves

Mix everything together & allow to sit at room temperature for 1 hour or more ~ strain some of the excess juice before serving. Pile mixture onto crisps, top with a fresh basil leaf. ♡

ASSORTED CROSTINI

The fun thing about crostini is how many ways they can be served — colors, textures & shapes — it's all up to you. Here are some ideas — start with crostini or fettunta recipes at left. ♥

Use soft goat cheese (Montrachet) as a base, & top it with a spoonful of pesto, or

Try rolling the cheese in toasted sesame seeds before broiling. ♥

Put a little piece of roasted red pepper on top, or

Spread crostini with roasted garlic & top with cherry tomato slices. ♥

Add slivers of sun-dried tomato,

Or just a sprinkle of fresh rosemary. ♥

Try long-cooked (caramelized) onions with a little slice of Gruyère cheese — broil. ♥

 Mix together ¼ c. mayonnaise, ¼ c. Parmesan cheese, & 2 Tbsp. minced red onion. Put a spoonful on crostini and broil till brown & bubbly. ♥

Try brie cheese topped with a slice of grilled Portobello mushroom (p. 57); broil till cheese melts. ♥

WHAT TO DO IN CASE OF EMERGENCY:
1. PICK UP YOUR HAT.
2. GRAB YOUR COAT.
3. LEAVE YOUR WORRIES ON THE DOORSTEP.
4. DIRECT YOUR FEET TO THE SUNNY SIDE OF THE STREET. ♥

GRILLED SAUSAGES
with APPLE SALSA

I think sausages are the perfect casual appetizer from the grill — you can cook them right along with the other food & cut off pieces to pop in the mouth as you go along. Or, be more formal & serve them with different mustards, spicy or sweet, tiny cornichon pickles & small hot sourdough rolls.

There are many delicious kinds of sausage available today including seafood. Try spiced chicken & turkey sausage (often available at gourmet food stores) & this salsa. ♥

3 Tbsp. sugar	3 sweet apples (Golden
1½ Tbsp. cider vinegar	Delicious) peeled,
1½ Tbsp. lemon juice	cored & chopped
¼ tsp. red pepper flakes	1 Tbsp. fresh oregano, minced
	(1 tsp. dried)

Stir sugar, vinegar, lemon juice & red pepper flakes together in small saucepan, bring to boil. Add chopped apple, cover pan & reduce heat; cook gently till apples are very soft. Mash them with a potato masher until practically smooth. Stir in oregano. Refrigerate, serve chilled. Makes 1½ c. ♥

PACIFIC COAST
PEELERS

More casual backyard dining ~ lay a thick layer of newspaper over the picnic table ~ pour the hot cooked shrimp right onto the paper ~ peel, dip & eat. ♥

2 lbs. med. shrimp, unpeeled   Heat beer to boiling. Add
beer to cover (about 3 12oz. cans)   shrimp, reduce heat &
cook 2-3 min. Do not overcook ~ shrimp should be opaque. Drain.
Serve with cocktail sauce (catsup, horseradish & lemon juice to taste).
Serves 6.

CLAM FRITTERS

MAKES 3 DOZ.
TINY FRITTERS

Canned clams are fine for this recipe
(and a lot faster than fresh!). ♥

2 - 6½ oz. cans minced
   clams
1 egg
2/3 c. flour
1 tsp. baking powder
½ tsp. Tabasco sauce
½ tsp. salt

3-4 grinds pepper
2 Tbsp. celery, minced
1 Tbsp. fresh parsley,
   minced
vegetable oil for frying
1 lemon } cut into
1 lime   } wedges

Preheat oven to 250° ~ put an oven-proof dish in
to get warm. Drain clams, reserve ⅓ c. liquid.
Beat egg in med. bowl, whisk in reserved liquid,
flour, baking powder, Tabasco, salt & pepper. Beat
well. Stir in clams, celery & parsley. Heat ½" oil
in large frying pan to med. high. Drop teaspoonfuls
of batter into hot oil (go easy ~ these should be tiny,
bite-sized); do not crowd pan. Cook on both sides,
drain on paper towels. Keep in warm oven till all
are done ~ serve on heated dish surrounded by
lemon & lime wedges. ♥

FARMERS' MARKET
Sugar Snap Peas & Salmon Dip

1½ lbs. sugar snap peas
6 oz. smoked salmon
1 c. sour cream

several drops Tabasco
1 tsp. capers
½ tsp. fresh dill, minced

Snap off top & bottom ends of sugar snap peas — pulling strings away. Bring 1½" water to boil in a large skillet. Add peas, cook 30 seconds, drain, refresh in cold water till cool. Chill well. Put smoked salmon, sour cream & Tabasco into food processor & blend until smooth, stir in capers & dill. Chill well. To serve put a small chilled bowl of dip on a pretty platter & arrange peas around it. ♥

Island Tomato Salsa
Makes 3 c.

5 med. vine-ripened tomatoes
½ tsp. salt
5 green onions, minced
1 jalapeño pepper, seeded & minced

2 tsp. minced cilantro
2 tsp. balsamic vinegar
2 tsp. olive oil
pepper & salt, to taste

Core & dice tomatoes into med. bowl — add salt & let sit ½ hour; pour off juice. Add green onions, jalapeño pepper (wash your hands after touching seeds), & rest of ingred. Chill. Serve with tacos, quesadillas, steak, fish, chicken, & chips. ♥

L ast night at twilight, we sat on the porch of an 18th century farm-house that looks out over Vineyard Haven Harbor — out from the kitchen came Laura with

NORTON FARM
TOMATOES & CHEVRE yes!

400° Serves 6 as appetizer

1 Tbsp. minced garlic
½ c. olive oil
2 lbs. cherry tomatoes
1 loaf focaccia bread (or French bread), heated

4 oz. soft, mild chevre (Montrachet) cheese
½ c. fresh basil, slivered

Sweet 100's are the best!

S teep garlic in olive oil at least ½ hr. Preheat oven to 400°. Wash & stem tomatoes & cut them in half. (Put unwrapped bread into oven.) Put tomatoes in a shallow baking dish, pour olive oil & garlic over & toss lightly. Bake 10 min.; sprinkle over chunks of cheese (cut into ½" pieces) & slivered basil. Stir gently. Serve with bread to mop up juices. ♥

ZUCCHINI STICKS

475° Serves 6

½ c. + 1 Tbsp. bread crumbs
¼ c. Parmesan
1½ tsp. fresh oregano, finely minced

3 med. zucchini
olive oil spray
freshly ground black pepper

P reheat oven to 475°. Combine bread crumbs, Parmesan & oregano on a plate. Cut squash into evenly sized spears. Put them on baking sheet in one layer, spray them with olive oil. Turn them all over & spray again. Roll each in crumbs mixture & back to oiled baking sheet. Bake 8-10 min. till brown. Serve hot. ♥

"A simple porch that stands alone, plain & shy-looking but full of romance...."
Marcel Proust ♥

SHRIMP FRA DIAVOLO

A perfect marriage of summer flavors ~ they're hot & spicy. Pass a dish of these around while you're waiting for the grill. I realize that canned tomatoes are almost blasphemy in the summer, but for this recipe the canned ones make it _so_ much easier & besides it's just too hot for peeling, seeding & dicing!

2 16 oz. cans peeled tomatoes, crushed & drained
2 lg. chopped onions (about 3 c.)
2 Tbsp. olive oil
4 large garlic cloves, crushed or minced
1/3 c. fresh basil, slivered
2 Tbsp. parsley, minced
1/4 tsp. red pepper flakes
20 extra-large shrimp, shelled (tails too) & deveined

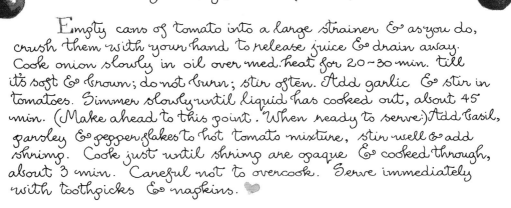

Empty cans of tomato into a large strainer & as you do, crush them with your hand to release juice & drain away. Cook onion slowly in oil over med. heat for 20~30 min. till it's soft & brown; do not burn; stir often. Add garlic & stir in tomatoes. Simmer slowly until liquid has cooked out, about 45 min. (Make ahead to this point. When ready to serve:) Add basil, parsley & pepper flakes to hot tomato mixture, stir well & add shrimp. Cook just until shrimp are opaque & cooked through, about 3 min. Careful not to overcook. Serve immediately with toothpicks & napkins.

" There's absolutely no reason for being rushed along with the rush. Everybody should be free to go very slow."

Robt. Frost

LONG LOAVES

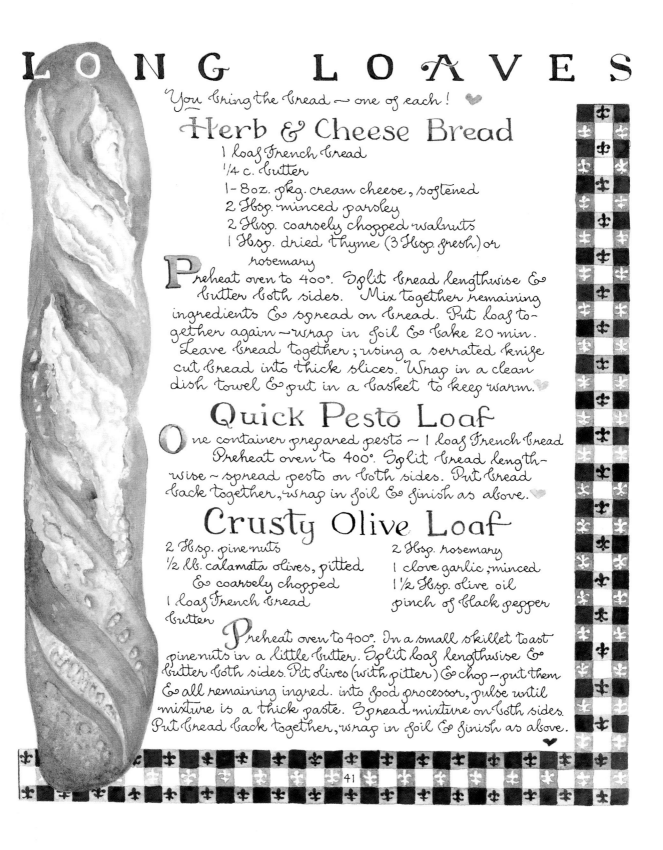

You bring the bread ~ one of each! 💛

Herb & Cheese Bread

1 loaf French bread
1/4 c. butter
1- 8oz. pkg. cream cheese, softened
2 Tbsp. minced parsley
2 Tbsp. coarsely chopped walnuts
1 Tbsp. dried thyme (3 Tbsp. fresh) or
    rosemary

Preheat oven to 400°. Split bread lengthwise & butter both sides. Mix together remaining ingredients & spread on bread. Put loaf together again ~ wrap in foil & bake 20 min. Leave bread together; using a serrated knife cut bread into thick slices. Wrap in a clean dish towel & put in a basket to keep warm. 💛

Quick Pesto Loaf

One container prepared pesto ~ 1 loaf French bread
    Preheat oven to 400°. Split bread lengthwise ~ spread pesto on both sides. Put bread back together, wrap in foil & finish as above. 💛

Crusty Olive Loaf

2 Tbsp. pine nuts
1/2 lb. calamata olives, pitted
    & coarsely chopped
1 loaf French bread
butter

2 Tbsp. rosemary
1 clove garlic; minced
1 1/2 Tbsp. olive oil
pinch of black pepper

Preheat oven to 400°. In a small skillet toast pine nuts in a little butter. Split loaf lengthwise & butter both sides. Pit olives (with pitter) & chop ~ put them & all remaining ingred. into food processor, pulse until mixture is a thick paste. Spread mixture on both sides. Put bread back together, wrap in foil & finish as above. 💛

Sandwiches

Spontaneity is a wonderful thing, so it's good to plan for it! For summer weekends you can make up a big plate of different sandwiches & you'll always be ready for a picnic, a trip to the beach, or the arrival of surprise guests. For extra cuteness, wrap them in waxed paper & stick on a decorative label to identify them. ♥ While trying new combinations, don't forget these old favorites:

Liverwurst on white bread with mustard, red onion, iceberg lettuce & thinly sliced cornichon pickles.

Egg Salad ~ hard-boiled eggs, mayo, pickle relish, minced celery & onion, celery seed, salt & pepper.

Tuna with potato chips; Cucumber. ♥

Cut good bread into heart, star, diamond, round & moon shapes. Decorate with delicate herbs & flowers.

Try egg salad with chives; nasturtium & cream cheese; or thin-sliced radishes & sweet butter.

SAVORY SCENTED SANDWICHES

Menu
Sandwiches
Peaches
Pink Lemonade

PANSY, ALSO KNOWN AS HEARTS-EASE, LOVE-IN-IDLENESS, TICKLE-MY-FANCY & KISS-HER-IN-THE PANTRY. TEA MADE FROM LEAVES CURES HEARTBREAK.

Or goat cheese with roasted red pepper & rosemary. Try goat cheese with sun-dried tomato & basil; sliced cherry tomato with bacon & cilantro mayonnaise. Decorate with borage blossoms, Johnny jump-ups, lemon zest, chive flowers or violets. ♥

A Portable Dinner

Picnic Sandwich

Eight portions

Pack this big, wonderful sandwich into a basket — add a good bottle of red wine, some chocolate-dipped strawberries & a thermos of iced coffee — plan a surprise picnic. ♥

Make Roasted Veggie Dressing, p. 31.

Cut a large round loaf of French bread (actually, any shape will do) in half & scoop out bread to make a cavity in each side. Rub inside of each half with cut garlic clove, sprinkle with a few drops of balsamic vinegar & sprinkle generously with olive oil — salt & pepper each side. Layer the following ingredients in the order given, more or less — feel free to add or subtract to your own tastes. 1. Start & end with slices of ripe garden tomatoes — 2. crumble on Montrachet cheese 3. sliced cucumber 4. roasted red peppers (p. 75) 5. grated carrots 6. a spoonful of dressing (p. 31) 7. sliced hard-boiled eggs 8. grilled tuna or swordfish 9. sprinkle on mashed anchovy 10. sliced radishes 11. roasted green beans (p. 74) 12. thin-sliced red onion 13. leaves of fresh basil or rosemary 14. another spoonful of dressing — finish up with more tomato slices. Wrap the sandwich tightly — put it on a plate with a heavy object on top — for at least 1 hour, turning once. Great served with beautiful sunset. ♥

A picnic is a state of mind & can be made anywhere.

BOLOGNA SANDWICHES & POTATO CHIPS

No one should have to live a whole life without tasting a correctly made bologna sandwich. Though they're not "politically correct," I've had countless & I'm healthy as can be. Here's how, in case you have forgotten :

Use soft white "bunny" bread, crisp <u>iceberg</u> lettuce, real mayonnaise, French's yellow mustard & bologna, of course. That's all, no pickles, no onions & it <u>has</u> to be iceberg. (Toast the bread only if you are out of potato chips.) Potato chips can be inserted into sandwich or eaten separately; include an orange cut into quarters, a glass of ice-cold milk & 2 Oreo cookies for dessert. If there's a Roy Rogers movie on TV you will have the perfect accompaniment ♥

"There are certain tastes which those who have never experienced them as children can neither understand nor cure : who but an Englishman, for example, can know the delights of stone-cold leathery toast for breakfast, or the wonders of 'Dead Man's Leg'?"

♥ W. H. Auden

45

Anatomy of a Cheeseburger McSue

(SHE LIKES 'EM JUICY)

1 - Start with a toasted sesame seed bun
2 - a big slice beefsteak tomato
3 - paper-thin slices red onion
4 - jack cheese well-melted over burger
5 - pink & juicy medium-rare hamburger
6 - crisp iceberg lettuce
7 - Of course, the secret sauce: mix together mayonnaise with just enough ketchup to turn it pink, a good amount of sweet pickle relish & lots of black pepper. Slather it on, if you please. ♥ Serve with potato salad (p. 68) & pickled veggies (p. 58) on a kind of bendy paper plate. Mmmmm, just right. ∵

♥   ♥   ♥

Tip: have you tried Garden Burgers & Smart Dogs yet? These are meatless hamburgers & hot dogs made of grains and veggies — they are truly delicious, <u>real food</u>, available in supermarkets & health food stores. ♥

FRESH FISH TACOS

I fell in love with these tacos last winter when I left our frozen harbor & below-zero temps & traveled to California. They were served outside at funky tables with umbrellas in a little fish joint near a tiny marina — the warm sun, clean air & sparkling sea soaked into my winter-raw psyche — the place was surrounded with flowers — I went every day! ♥

For each serving:
a large flour tortilla
1/4 lb. fresh fish: monkfish, swordfish,
    red snapper, scallops (in bite-sized pieces)
shredded iceberg lettuce
grated jack cheese
fresh tomato salsa (p. 38)

Wrap the tortilla in tin foil & place in 350° oven for 10 min. Meanwhile cook the fish: steam it in just a bit of water, grill it, or fry it in butter or oil just until done (opaque). Put the warm tortilla on a plate, then the fresh fish, cover with lettuce, sprinkle over a little cheese & spoon on some fresh salsa. ♥

"I'm trying to arrange my life so
that I don't even have to be
present." ♥ Anonymous

47

"The Sun and Fog contested The Government of Day —
The Sun took down his Yellow Whip And drove the Fog away."
— EMILY DICKINSON

VEGETABLE BAGUETTE

Hot, crunchy, good for you.

1 French bread baguette per person   sliced tomato
Dijon mustard   thinly sliced red onion
mayonnaise (opt.)   thinly sliced cucumber
½ c. grated carrot   shredded lettuce

Heat oven to 350°. Put unwrapped baguettes in to warm — about 10 min. Split, spread with Dijon & mayonnaise (if you like) & rest of ingredients.

STEAK TACOS

For 4

Forget those little ground-meat dealie-bobs, here's the real thing!

4 flour tortillas
1 lb. beef steak (flank or top sirloin)
salt & freshly ground pepper
2 c. diced tomatoes
1 c. sour cream
2 Tbsp. minced cilantro (opt.)

Warm tortillas (in microwave or in the oven, wrapped in foil). Thinly slice steak — quickly sauté slices in a lightly oiled hot skillet till just brown, but pink in the middle. Put beef on hot tortilla, s. & p., diced tomato, sour cream & cilantro.

ROLL UP + EAT, DRIPPINGLY, & WITH RELISH.

Soft-Shell Crab Sandwich
Serves Four

You can use any fried fresh fish for this. ♥

Tartar Sauce (below)
4 soft-shell crabs
flour for dredging
Cajun seasoning or cayenne pepper (opt.)

vegetable oil for frying
4 soft hamburger buns, heated
1½ c. shredded lettuce

Tartar Sauce

1 c. mayonnaise
1 Tbsp. capers
1 Tbsp. minced
  parsley
2 tsp. minced green
  onion
2 tsp. minced sweet
  pickle
1½ Tbsp. cider vinegar
Blend ingred. & chill.

Make Tartar Sauce. Preheat oven to 350°. Rinse & dry the crabs. Mix flour with a little season- ing if you like & put it into a shallow dish. Heat ½" oil in a large skillet ~ very hot. Put buns in oven to warm. Dredge the crabs in flour & fry them hot & fast, about 2 min. each side, till brown & crisp. Drain on paper towels. Divide lettuce between bottom buns; top each with a Tbsp. of Tartar Sauce, a crab & top bun. Delicious served with a little pile of French fried onion rings.

Onion Rings
2 lg. yellow onions; 1 c. milk; ¼ c. flour; vegetable oil. Cut onions into thin slices; separate into rings. Soak them in milk ½ hr. Heat 1" oil ~ dredge rings in flour heavily ~ fry till golden, a few at a time. Drain on paper towels; sprinkle with salt. Keep warm in 250° oven & serve. ♥

A LITTLE NIGHT MUSIC

LOST IN THE STARS

HOW HIGH THE MOON

I DIDN'T KNOW WHAT TIME IT WAS

Simple but Elegant MIDNIGHT SUPPER UNDER THE STARS

Lie back on the sand or grass & watch the stars fall — look for the Big Dipper & the Milky Way. Get a blanket & your sweetheart & take along this romantic picnic — heavenly! ♡

Champagne

Montrachet Cheese & Green Grapes
Crusty French Bread Baguette

Cold Lobsters
and/or
Sliced Prime Rib & Country Mustard
Potato Salad

Chocolate-Dipped Strawberries

Thermos of Coffee

SOME ENCHANTED EVENING

IN THE STILL OF THE NIGHT

THE NIGHT THEY INVENTED CHAMPAGNE

I COULD HAVE DANCED ALL NIGHT

OLD DEVIL MOON

IT'S ONLY A PAPER MOON

AS WE SING LOVE'S OLD SWEET SONG ON MOONLIGHT BAY

MOONGLOW

SHALL WE DANCE?

LIGHTING

W hen we eat supper under the rose arbor, the greatest enjoyments (after the food!) are the fireflies, the starlight & the moon. For dinner parties we try enhancing that mood by covering the arbor in tiny white lights & decorating with every candle we can find. At one party we even had little fireworks & sparklers with dessert. Quite dazzling — a real "light show." Special lighting can make magic — here are some other ideas:

Flaming tiki torches look wild & crazy & if you have a luau, they're a must!

We have a giant 3-dimensional tin star with cut-outs all over & a light inside that makes a great "chandelier" over the picnic table.

Japanese lanterns are lovely & delicate when lit from inside — hang them from trees & night-picnic under them.

Luminarias are perfect to light the way — down a path, wherever you want to go or be.

Colored tea lights hung on fences or between tree branches; oil lanterns & candles in clear or colored glass will make a party sparkle.

 THE RAFT

Looking back, I'd guess that summer was most likely a trying time for my mother — eight children home all day in 90° weather had to have its moments. I spent almost every summer at the public library — for more reasons than one — it was air-conditioned & they let us go barefooted in there! But my brothers had bigger fish to fry & one summer the project was "the raft."

I don't know where they got the boards, but I saw them arrive with them. They had one guy on a bike pedaling like mad & behind him, tied to the bike with ropes, were 1, 2, 3 red wagons, like a train. The boards were strung across the wagons in a pile, and the other boys ran alongside making sure they didn't lose anything along the way. My brothers were brilliant.

There was a small man-made pond in a nearby park that was stocked with teeny little fish that we would fish for on summer mornings. This pond was the intended christening area. The boys (which included more than just ours — we lived in a neighborhood full of giant families) worked industriously on their project. They used a lot of nails.

Finally the big day came — the raft was done & it was huge. It took half the neighborhood to load it onto my dad's 1947 Ford pickup; they all climbed aboard & my mom drove everyone to the park. They heaved & hauled this beast across the park & finally got it to the pond. Confidently, they pushed & shoved their masterpiece into the water, where it sank like a concrete block — it didn't even look back — it was gone.

There was a long moment of shock — then a discussion of possible rescue — rusty fish hooks & years of duck guck on the bottom made rescue look unfun. So my mom, being on top of things at all times, took them down to the drugstore to drown their sorrows in ice cream.

The day has never been a total loss because now we have this story to tell at every family gathering & it always rocks the house with laughter. What a great raft. ♥

SIDE DISHES

Veggies · Casseroles · Soups · Salads · Dressings

" I am painting now with the rapture of a Marseillais eating bouillabaisse, which will not surprise you when you hear that the subject is big sunflowers. I am working on them every morning, starting at daybreak — for they fade quickly...."
♥ Vincent van Gogh

Simple Side Dish Ideas

White Rice Salad: Simple & perfect; serves 8. 3 c. white rice; 1/4 c. white wine vinegar, 2 Tbsp. vegetable oil; 2 Tbsp. fresh lemon juice; 1 Tbsp. fresh dill; 1 tsp. salt; freshly ground pepper. Cook rice & toss lightly with all other ingredients. Chill. ♥

With a 1" cutter, cut stars out of cooked beets, carrots, red pepper, or jicama to add to 4th of July salads. ♥

Stuffed Cherry Tomatoes: Make tiny orzo pasta, mix with pesto. Hollow out cherry tomatoes & drain them on paper towels. Fill each with pesto pasta. ♥

Coleslaw: quick & easy. Buy shredded cabbage, or finely shred your own, purple & green. Add grated carrots & a can or two of crushed pineapple (reserve juice). Mix together mayonnaise & enough reserved juice to make a nice consistency; pour over cabbage, sprinkle over sliced almonds, toss. Chill. ♥

Sliced Tomatoes: When tomatoes come in season, cut beefsteak tomatoes in thick slices. On a large platter, overlap with slices of mozzarella cheese & thinly sliced red onion. Drizzle a little olive oil over all, grind over pepper, a little salt & sprinkle over slivered fresh basil. Best at room temp. ♥

In my other cookbooks I have some recipes especially suited to summer, so don't forget about: Avocado Soup, Gazpacho, Cioppino, Ceviche, Bean Salad, Pesto, Greek Potato Salad, Pasta Salad, Summer Salad with Rosemary, & Tabbouli. ♥

"I believe in festival days with all my heart. I think we should sometimes call our friends together, and give them bright thoughts for the intellect, friendliness for the heart, and good things for the palate." ♥ A.M.Diaz

POTATO PIE

375° Makes 8 servings

We had this for dinner last night & we decided that to be honest I should say it "Serves 2." ☺ Great at potlucks ! ♥ Make it early, bake just before serving.

5 med. Idaho potatoes	3 Tbsp. minced fresh chives
3 Tbsp. butter	1¼ tsp. salt
3 Tbsp. flour	lots of freshly ground pepper
1 c. milk	1 c. grated sharp cheddar
¼ c. minced parsley	cheese

Butter a 10" pie plate. Peel, quarter & cook potatoes in a large saucepan in salted boiling water until fork-tender. Drain (in colander). In same pan, melt butter, whisk in flour till blended & bubbly. Pour in milk & whisk constantly till thickened. Remove from heat. On a dinner plate (for easy cleanup), slice potatoes thinly (¼ in.) & add them (and all the crumbs) to the saucepan; add parsley, 2 Tbsp. of chives, salt & pepper. Stir gently. Spread mixture in prepared pan & refrigerate till serving time. When ready, preheat oven to 375°. Sprinkle cheese evenly over pie & bake 30-35 min. till golden, toasty brown. Sprinkle over remaining 1 Tbsp. chives & serve. ♥

"Life itself is the proper binge."
♥ Julia Child

"LOVE APPLE" PIE

BAKED TOMATO SALAD

475°

Serve chilled in the baking dish as a salad, or even as an appetizer, but be sure to have some hot crusty bread to mop up the delicious tomato juices. ♥

olive oil
large, ripe summer tomatoes
salt & freshly ground pepper
minced fresh parsley
minced fresh basil (or cilantro)
1 jar roasted red peppers (or homemade,
    if you're so inclined), chopped
dry bread crumbs
capers

Choose a heavy baking dish   for number of servings you desire. Preheat oven to 475°. Put a   good film of olive oil in the bottom of your dish. Cut the tomatoes in 1/4" slices & put a single layer into the baking dish. Salt & pepper lightly — sprinkle over a pinch of parsley, a pinch of basil, then a layer of sliced roasted red peppers. Repeat the process, tomatoes, condiments, peppers. Add one more layer of tomatoes & condiments. Drizzle over a little olive oil, cover lightly with bread crumbs & sprinkle with capers. Bake 20 min. Chill well before serving. ♥

GRILLED PORTOBELLO MUSHROOM SALAD

To vegetarians, Portobello mushrooms are as close to steak as they're going to get. Some of them are bigger than my spread hand — they have a deep, dark, woodsy flavor & wonderful texture when grilled. I also steam them, sliced, in only balsamic vinegar. They are so flavorful I rarely even use a salad dressing. Ask your grocer to get them for you. ♥

Rub a wooden salad bowl with a cut garlic clove. Make a big beautiful salad with as many kinds of fresh greens as you can, including spinach, romaine, curly endive, etc. Gently tear greens, don't cut them or wring them. Include chopped & whole herbs like parsley, tarragon, chives, basil and/or thyme; some toasted nuts such as walnuts, pine nuts, or sliced almonds & some flowers such as nasturtiums, Johnny jump-ups, or borage flowers. Toss with Hot Mustard Vinaigrette just before serving (if you like).

Brush the mushrooms with a mixture of half balsamic vinegar & half olive oil — grill them over hot coals until tender — then give them a good grind of pepper. Cut the mushrooms into thick slices, bring out the salad bowl, lay hot mushrooms over greens & serve. ♥

Hot Mustard Vinaigrette

3 slices bacon
1 Tbsp. minced shallot
2 Tbsp. brown sugar

1 Tbsp. Dijon mustard
1/4 c. balsamic vinegar
1/2 c. olive oil

Fry bacon till crisp & remove from pan. Pour off all but 1 Tbsp. fat; sauté shallots, whisk in brown sugar, Dijon, vinegar & oil. Remove from heat & cool slightly. Crumble bacon over salad & toss with dressing. ♥

FIREWORKS

PICKLED VEGETABLES
Serves 4

Color is spectacular, vegetables cold, clean & crisp — a spicy, crazy flavor, great side dish! ♥

1 large carrot	1 c. white cabbage, shredded
½ yellow pepper	1 c. white vinegar
½ red pepper	1 tbsp. sugar
8 green beans	1 tsp. minced fresh ginger
½ c. cauliflower florets	

Prepare veggies: peel & cut carrot into matchstick-size pieces. Seed peppers & also cut into matchsticks. Top & tail beans, halve or third them. Break cauliflower into tiny florets. Shred cabbage. Put all but cabbage into glass casserole dish. In a small non-aluminum saucepan bring to boil vinegar, sugar & ginger. Pour over vegetables, stir well & add cabbage. Refrigerate & stir occasionally for at least 3 hrs. before serving ♥. Good with broccoli, jicama, daikon radish, your call.

RED BEANS
Serves 6

You need them with steak, burgers, chicken, ribs — like Mom, the flag & apple pie, ya gotta have beans. ♥

½ lb. red chili (or kidney) beans	3/4 tsp. salt
½ c. chopped onion	½ tsp. cumin
¼ c. tomato puree	¼ tsp. ground red pepper
2 cloves garlic, minced	¼ c. sour cream
1 bay leaf	1 med. red onion, chopped

Rinse & drain beans; put them in pot with water to cover. Bring to boil, cover, turn off heat, let sit 1 hr. Drain, rinse again, return to saucepan with 3 c. water & next 7 ingred. Bring to boil, reduce heat, cover & simmer 2½ hrs., stirring occasionally. Uncover, cook 20 min. Remove bay leaf. Top with sour cream & onions & serve. ♥

S K E W E R E D
NEW POTATOES
and FENNEL

Serves 6

2 lb. new potatoes
2 lb. fennel
¼ c. olive oil
1 Tbsp. minced fresh parsley

1 tsp. dried thyme leaves
1 tsp. salt
lots of freshly ground pepper

If using wooden skewers, put about 15 in a glass of water to soak. Halve potatoes & boil till just tender, drain. Remove leaves from fennel bulbs. Cut in half & then around stalk diagonally into chunks about the size of potato halves — hold the little chunks together in one piece by piercing them through with toothpicks. Drop them into boiling water, cook until tender, drain. Combine remaining ingredients, except pepper, in a small bowl. Thread potatoes & fennel (remove toothpicks) onto skewers — put them on a cookie sheet. Brush oil mixture over potatoes & fennel, turning as you go. Grind pepper over. Grill over high heat till edges brown & char slightly ~ 15-20 min. You can also cook them in a preheated 475° oven, but they taste best from the grill. ♥

SWEET CORN

400°   8 ears of corn

8 ears fresh corn
½ c. softened butter (1 Tbsp. ea.)

3 Tbsp. minced parsley (1 tsp. ea.)
salt & freshly ground pepper

Husk corn. Combine butter & parsley. Lay out 8 pieces of aluminum foil. Butter corn well, salt & pepper, wrap each in foil. Bake at 400° for 20 min. ♥

WHITE BEAN SALAD

Serves 6

A spoonful or two of this will perk up any green salad. You can make it with or without the tuna — good both ways. ❤

½ lb. small white beans (dried)
1 c. celery, chopped
¾ c. red onion, minced
½ c. fresh parsley, chopped
2 tsp. dried oregano (1½ tbsp. fresh)
1 6 oz. can tuna packed in water, drained (opt.)
Niçoise olives, opt.

Rinse & drain beans. Bring them to a boil in 3 c. water. Reduce heat, simmer 5 min. Remove from heat, cover & let sit 1 hr. Rinse beans & return to pan with 8 c. fresh water. Simmer 20 min. so beans are tender, but not mushy. Rinse in cold water. Make dressing. Combine all ingred. & chill. Scatter olives over.

Dressing: combine all ingredients.
4 tbsp. olive oil; 4 tbsp. red wine vinegar; 3 sm. garlic cloves, pressed; 2 anchovies, finely minced; ½ tsp. salt, lots o' pepper.

Dog days: START MID-JULY, END LABOR DAY — THE DOG STAR SIRIUS RISES & SETS WITH THE SUN.

Free as a bird
Brown as a berry

"MY NAME IS MARGALO," SAID THE BIRD, SOFTLY, IN A MUSICAL VOICE. "I COME FROM FIELDS ONCE TALL WITH WHEAT,

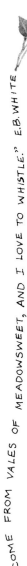
"I COME FROM VALES OF MEADOWSWEET, AND I LOVE TO WHISTLE." E.B.WHITE

RASPBERRY SOUP

Serves 4

In the winter I cook pears in red wine & cinnamon for an elegant dessert & in the summer I use raspberries for this ice-cold soup with sophisticated flavor. ♥

4 - 10 oz. pkgs. frozen raspberries (in juice), thawed

2 c. good red wine (Cabernet Sauvignon)

9 inches of cinnamon sticks

2 tsp. cornstarch

1 pt. vanilla ice cream

Put raspberries, wine & cinnamon sticks in a saucepan; bring to boil, reduce heat & simmer gently 15 min. Mix cornstarch with ½ c. water & gradually stir into soup; cook until thickened; cover & chill. When cold, remove cinnamon sticks & press soup (in batches) through a sieve with a wooden spoon to remove seeds. To serve, put 3-4 melonballers-full of ice cream in each bowl & add soup. ♥

FROM PASTURES DEEP IN FERN AND THISTLE;

61

GRACE ❂ HAPPENS

HOW I WISH THAT SOMEWHERE THERE EXISTED AN ISLAND FOR THOSE
THAT ARE WISE AND OF GOOD WILL.   ALBERT EINSTEIN

The "happening" bumper sticker this summer — conceived by Tricia Newell, executed with panache by her 9 yr. old pal Russell Hodson.

CHEESE & GREEN CHILI POLENTA

350° Serves 4

Polenta is the current word for corn grits — call it what you want, grits is what you get; this easy casserole goes great with all summer foods; just double the recipe for a large group. ♥

2 tbsp. butter	1/4 tsp. cumin
1 tbsp. flour	1/8 tsp. cayenne
2 c. milk	1/4 c. chopped green onions
1 c. corn grits *	1/2 c. grated jack cheese
1 4 1/2 oz. can chopped green chilies	

Preheat oven to 350°. *Corn grits are available at health food stores. Melt butter in saucepan. Stir in flour. Over med. heat, slowly add milk, then grits. Stir until thick. Add chilies, cumin, cayenne & green onions. Pour into buttered baking dish — sprinkle cheese over the top. Bake 40 min. Serve hot. ♥

"There are strange evenings
when the flowers have a soul."
Albert Samain

CANTALOUPE SOUP

GORGEOUS COLOR

GARNISH WITH BORAGE FLOWERS OR MINT LEAVES

Serves 4

1 large, ripe cantaloupe
1 c. fresh orange juice
½ c. plain yogurt
1 Tbsp. fresh lime juice

Cut cantaloupe in half, remove seeds, scoop out flesh & put it into blender along with all other ingredients. Blend till smooth. Chill well & garnish with flowers. ♥

"The dandelions and buttercups
gild all the lawn; the drowsy bee
stumbles among the clover tops,
and summer sweetens all to me."
♥ J. R. Lowell

WEST CHOP CORN

350° Serves 6

What makes this West Chop corn is the cream, of course. ♥ You don't *have* to wear lime green pants with spouting whales all over them in order to enjoy this dish, but it *does* help. :) Great sidedish for a cookout. ♥ Perfect with martinis!

3 c. fresh corn cut off the cob
2/3 c. heavy cream
1 tsp. dried thyme leaves
pinch of cayenne
salt & pepper
1/4 c. + 2 Tbsp. fresh bread crumbs
3 Tbsp. Parmesan cheese

Stir together corn, cream, thyme & cayenne. Pour mixture into a buttered baking dish, grind pepper over, sprinkle lightly with salt. Mix together bread crumbs & Parmesan cheese & sprinkle over corn. Bake in preheated 350° oven for 30 min. till topping is browned. Serve hot. ♥

Lost in Paradise

Finding your way around the island isn't easy because for the most part there aren't any addresses (or any street signs for that matter). So, directions are "head out to West Chop & go left at the painted rock." In the summer, one Edgartown family nails a small striped T-shirt to a tree near their house ~ it means "turn here." Our street names are colorful too ~ we have Music St., Meeting House Way & Tea Lane, to name a few. But my favorite of all is the one officially called "Dirt Road." You'd have to live here to know that ~ there's no sign! ♥

As I was boning up on my Fried Green Tomato recipe for this book, I found myself explaining this dish to someone from another country. Suddenly I was reminded of a quote from The Eskimo Cookbook for Loon Soup: "Do Not Make Loon Soup". That's pretty much how I feel about fried green tomatoes. No matter how thick & crunchy the coating, no matter how cunning you are with the Fryolater, still at the bottom of it all are green tomatoes, which by definition are tomatoes that aren't ready to be eaten because they aren't ripe yet. I know that the recipe originated when our foremothers scooped up the last of the tomatoes before the first frost came in, then, being the thrifty, creative women they were (always looking to make lemonade when life dealt them lemons), they happened upon a way, they thought, to make green tomatoes palatable. They fed them to their children, probably playing all the food games to get them to eat them: zooming, smacking lips, mmmmmmming, and voilà (!) we had a dish that became "a dish of our childhood" — which elevated it to the level of "Dead Man's Leg" (see quote on p. 45). Now it's like folklore & the recipes appear in Gourmet magazine & all the best cookbooks. What can I say? Far be it from me to deny anyone their childhood food loves — after all, I'm the one who put Bologna Sandwiches in this book. So here's for you who love

FRIED GREEN TOMATOES

SERVES 4

2/3 c. yellow cornmeal; 2 tbsp. brown sugar; 2 lg. green tomatoes; 2 eggs, beaten; 1/2 c. flour. Mix together cornmeal & sugar. Cut tomatoes in 1/4" slices. Beat eggs; put flour in another dish. Dip tomatoes: egg - flour - egg - cornmeal. Fry till brown in veg. oil. Serve with s. & p. & lemon wedges. (BETTER YET, JUST READ THE BOOK)

Fisher Farm Picnic Squash Salad

Serves 10

In summer we're busy—we often feel "the need for speed." Here's an easy salad—beautiful & delicious— that doesn't *sound* anywhere <u>near</u> how great it actually <u>is</u> ♥

8 c. very thinly sliced squash, any kind *yellow crookneck AND green zucchini= pretty!*
2 c. Paul Newman's salad dressing
20 fresh nasturtium blossoms
2 Tbsp. fresh herb of choice (opt.)

Put the squash into a large bowl. Bring salad dressing to near boil—pour over squash, toss lightly & then chill. Before serving toss again— pour off extra dressing. Toss again with fresh herbs & top with fresh nasturtiums. ♥

"EARTH LAUGHS IN FLOWERS."
♥ Ralph Waldo Emerson

SPICY ORANGE BROCCOLI

Serves 4

Here's a recipe for broccoli even ex-presidents would like (you know who you are :) . ♥

3 tbsp. olive oil
2 cloves minced garlic
1 tbsp. minced shallot
peeled rind of 1 orange, chopped
  (no white pith)
⅛ tsp. red pepper flakes

1 large bunch of broccoli
  (cut in florets)
⅓ c. orange juice
1 tsp. balsamic vinegar
¼ tsp. salt
¼ tsp. sesame oil

Sauté first 5 ingredients in large frying pan over medium heat till garlic & shallots have softened, stirring frequently. (Broccoli should be cut in fairly uniform pieces so they all take about the same time to cook.) Add broccoli to pan; cook & stir 1 min. Add orange juice, vinegar & salt. Cover, steam 3-4 min. over med-high heat till desired doneness. Drizzle with sesame oil. Toss & serve hot, OR it's just as delicious (maybe more) chilled & served cold. ♥

"It is perhaps a more fortunate destiny to have a taste for collecting shells than to be born a millionaire."
♥ Robert Louis Stevenson

POTATO SALAD

Serves 10-12

Every family thinks their potato salad recipe is the BEST. I've put some really great but less traditional potato salad recipes in my other books, but this is the one we ate at home. Old-fashioned, the mayo melts into the hot potatoes & eggs & makes bowl-licking de rigueur! If your family hasn't hooked up with a potato salad worth fighting for, try ours, which is. ♥

7 large Idaho potatoes
7 eggs
2 c. mayonnaise
1 3/4 c. minced red onion
3/4 c. sweet pickle relish
3-4 celery stalks, diced
1 tsp. celery seed
1/2 tsp. salt (or to taste)
lots of freshly ground black pepper

Peel potatoes, halve them & drop them into a big pot of boiling water & cook till fork tender. Meanwhile, hard boil eggs. Peel them, put them in a big bowl & mash them with a potato masher to the chunkiness you like them to be. Drain potatoes, cut them into bite-sized pieces & add to bowl along with other ingredients — stir gently. Chill. ♥

TIP: Starch will come right off pan or colander if you use COLD water to wash or soak in.

ALL THE FLOWERS OF ALL THE TOMORROWS ARE IN THE SEEDS OF TODAY. ♥

CHEESE ROASTED POTATOES

350° Serves 6

6 large baking potatoes
¼ c. butter
½ tsp. salt
½ c. finely grated cheddar cheese

¼ c. minced chives or green onion
3 tbsp. dry bread crumbs
1 tbsp. Parmesan cheese
freshly ground pepper

Preheat oven to 350°. Melt butter. Peel & dry potatoes. Cut a thin slice off long side of potatoes so they sit flat. Cut vertical slits from top <u>almost</u> to bottom of each potato. Place them on cookie sheet, brush them with melted butter, salt & bake 1½ hrs., basting occasionally with remaining butter. Combine cheeses, chives (or green onion) & bread crumbs. Remove potatoes from oven, allow to cool slightly. Set oven to broil. Carefully fill slits with cheese mixture — sprinkle any remaining over tops. Sprinkle with pepper. Broil until golden brown — watch closely. Serve. ♥

"The highlight of my childhood was making my brother laugh so hard that food came out his nose."
♥ Garrison Keillor

"The town where I grew up had a zip code of E-I-E-I-O."
Martin Mull ♥

LEMON LINGUINI

Serves 6

This is your basic summer pasta, wonderful just plain & simple, even good cold. You can add a variety of things to make it "more" — for instance: steamed shrimp & asparagus spears; roasted green beans & grilled chicken strips; or chopped tomatoes, slivered fresh basil & toasted pine nuts. ♥

1 lb. linguini   ½ c. chopped green onion
½ c. olive oil   ¼ c. chopped fresh parsley
zest from 1 lemon   salt & freshly ground pepper
juice from 2 lemons   lots of Parmesan cheese

Cook linguini in boiling salted water till done; drain well. Combine next 5 ingred. in a large serving bowl. Add pasta & toss well. Sprinkle over salt & freshly ground pepper — toss in Parmesan to taste. Serve, or toss in additional ingred. of your choice. ♥

Sweet Nights

Even though I really didn't like them, I used to eat Sugar Daddys on the nights we slept out in the backyard. We all did. We tested all candy & Sugar Daddys won because they lasted longest — so if one of us had one we all had to have them if we were to be truly happy those long, damp summer nights spent in sleeping bags, scanning the sky for falling stars, till our EYES were full of stars. The real trick was to stay awake long enough to finish that sucker! ☆

PARSLEY SALAD

Serves 6

If you are what you eat, then eat this ~ kind of an unprocessed pesto, fresh & bright, spicy, curly, & full of personality. Especially suited to tomatoes (with cottage cheese ~ yum!).

2-3 cloves garlic, peeled & pressed
1/2 c. olive oil
2 Tbsp. balsamic vinegar
salt & freshly ground pepper
6 c. parsley, stemmed & torn into pieces
1/2 c. grated Parmesan

Put garlic through garlic press & combine with oil, vinegar & salt & pepper. One hour before serving, pour dressing over parsley (which should have been previously washed & allowed to dry), toss with Parmesan. Cover & chill until serving time. ♥

"ONE YEAR MY HUSBAND AND I RENTED A LAKE COTTAGE —
A RUSTIC CABIN SET IN A PINE GROVE JUST A STROLL FROM
THE LAKE. WITH THIS COTTAGE CAME A WAR CANOE AND A
SCREENED-IN PORCH. THE MOTTO OF THE OWNERS SEEMED TO
HAVE BEEN 'IT'S BROKEN! LET'S TAKE IT TO THE LAKE!'"
♥ Laurie Colwin

SUNSHINE SALAD

Serves 6

2 lbs. carrots, peeled & grated
1 c. raisins
1 c. coarsely chopped walnuts
1 c. mayonnaise
2 Tbsp. fresh lemon juice

Peel carrots, grate them, put them in a big bowl. Add all other ingredients & mix well. Chill. ♥

"THE SUNSHINE SEEMED TO BLESS, THE AIR WAS A CARESS." ♥ John Greenleaf Whittier

NEW LANE PEAS

Serves 6

2 10 oz. pkgs. frozen baby peas
1 c. chopped celery
1/2 c. coarsely chopped cashew nuts
2 green onions, minced
1/2 c. sour cream

1/2 tsp. dried oregano
1/4 tsp. garlic salt
salt & pepper
4 slices bacon, crisp cooked & crumbled (opt.)

Thaw peas in a colander. Gently combine all ingredients except bacon. Cook bacon & drain on paper towels. Crumble over salad & chill well. ♥

". . . THAT SUN-DAPPLED, BONNY NEW LANE." ♥

72

Fresh corn Salad

Makes 8 cups

This is a perfect big salad to take to a picnic or barbecue — colorful & delicious with anything from the grill. ♥

6 ears of sweet corn
1 yellow pepper, chopped

1 red pepper, chopped
1 red onion, minced

½ c. cilantro, chopped
¼ c. lime juice

¼ c. olive oil
salt & pepper to taste

Cut the fresh corn off the cob & steam for 3-5 min. in ¼ c. water. Remove lid & cook, stirring, 2 min. more till water evaporates. Toss corn with all other ingredients & chill. ♥

How to Roast Vegetables

Roasted vegetables go great with anything from the grill — I also love them in a green salad or on a pizza — when you make them, make extra!

Rosemary Potatoes

Preheat oven to 400°. Brush a baking sheet with olive oil. Cut small red potatoes in half (or large potatoes into pieces). Dip cut surfaces into a mixture of fresh rosemary leaves, salt & cracked pepper & lay them face down on baking sheet. Brush with olive oil & bake till toasted brown — 30 min. For spicier potato try using Cajun seasoning salt.

Green Beans

Preheat oven to 450°. Wash & trim beans — allow them to dry. Spread on baking sheet, drizzle lightly with olive oil & toss them to distribute oil — grind over black pepper. Bake 15-20 min. till soft & starting to brown; turn them occasionally. Sprinkle with salt.

Roasted Garlic & Shallots

Preheat oven to 350°. Do not remove paper skins — except if they're loose. Toss with olive oil. Bake shallots ½ hr; garlic for 1 hr. Stir occasionally. They'll slip right out of their skins ♥.

All roasted vegetables taste best warm or at room temp.

Roasted Carrots

Preheat oven to 400°. Use skinny carrots or cut them in half lengthwise. Peel them & dry them. Baste lightly with olive oil, grind over black pepper & bake on a cookie sheet for about ½ hr. until carrots are soft & starting to brown.

Roasted Red Peppers

Heat the broiler. Place whole peppers on a baking sheet & as close to flame as possible. Allow skin to blacken, turn when needed. Remove from oven & close them into a brown paper bag to steam. When cool, remove core, seeds & peel, but don't wash them. Slice them into wide strips. Use them in salads, on sand-wiches & pizza. A bowlful of them mixed with a little garlic, minced parsley, olive oil & black pepper — served with French bread & baked chevre & a good glass of red wine — makes a perfect little picnic. ♥

"Long live the sun which gives us such color."

♥ Paul Cézanne

SUNSHINE TOMATO DRESSING

Tastes of summer & the sun, this recipe goes a long way.
Delicious over mixed greens & soft goat cheese as a salad
dressing; break up chunks of good & dense day-old French
bread & it's a Tuscan bread salad (add olives, sliced red
onion & cucumber), & it is terrific over linguini too!
(Especially when you add a few chunks of lobster, some
Parmesan cheese & maybe a wee side of that yummy cold
Baked Tomato Salad on p. 56 . YES YES YES !) ♡

Put all ingred. in a glass bowl or jar, cover tightly & set it in
the sun for 4-5 hrs. Keep in the fridge but serve at room temp.

8 vine-ripened garden tomatoes,   ¼ c. balsamic vinegar
    roughly chopped   2 Tbsp. fresh basil, slivered
3 cloves garlic, put through press   2 Tbsp. parsley, chopped
3 shallots, chopped   1 tsp. sugar
1 c. good, fruity olive oil   lots of pepper; salt to taste

"THEY AREN'T LONG, THE DAYS OF WINE AND ROSES!" ♡ E. DOWSON

SALAD DRESSINGS

Raspberry Dressing

Makes 1 cup

½ c. salad oil

3 Tbsp. raspberry vinegar

1 Tbsp. raspberry jam

1 Tbsp. minced shallots

½ Tbsp. Dijon mustard

a few fresh raspberries

Whisk everything together — great on fresh spinach. ♥

Anchovy Mustard Dressing

Makes 1 cup

4 anchovy fillets, rinsed

4 whole cloves

2 green onions, minced

4 leaves basil, slivered

2 Tbsp. minced parsley

2 cloves garlic, garlic pressed

⅛ tsp. cayenne pepper

1 Tbsp. Dijon mustard

2 Tbsp. balsamic vinegar

¾ c. olive oil

Soak the rinsed anchovies for 1 hr. in a little water with the cloves. Remove anchovies, finely mince & combine with next 7 ingred. Gradually whisk in olive oil in a thin stream. ♥

Magic Garlic Cream

Makes 1 cup

½ c. milk

½ c. sour cream

2 tsp. olive oil

1 clove garlic, pressed

2 tsp. cider vinegar

salt & pepper, to taste

Whisk all ingred. together in order given. ♥

How to Draw

Drawing is a lot easier than you might think. I got a late start in drawing & painting because I never tried & I never imagined I could do it. I finally painted my first picture at age 30 — what a happy & completely unexpected surprise that was! Up till then my creative outlets were sewing, embroidery & cooking — I got an A in 7th grade art, but it was an elective & I thought everybody got an A! Confidence & belief in yourself is everything I've learned since then. After all, some people can draw — why shouldn't one of them be you?

So here's how to start: get a little drawing pad, a sharp #2 pencil, a soft eraser & a pencil sharpener. Put something in front of you that you like — I started with a potted geranium. Choose a place on your subject to begin. Use your eyes to measure distances between different points. For a pot you can start by drawing a guideline down the middle of the page & do your best to make everything on both sides of the line equal. (Feel free to erase profusely.) You can use your finger to smear the pencil to make shadows.

Try it, you might like it, and you do get better as you go along! What I loved most was getting all this "free" artwork for my walls! Nothing has to be perfect; if you can draw, you can paint — color is fun & being creative is good for the soul. ♥

"NOTHING FEEDS THE CENTER OF BEING SO MUCH AS CREATIVE WORK. THE CURTAIN OF MECHANIZATION HAS COME DOWN BETWEEN THE MIND AND THE HAND." ♥ ANNE MORROW LINDBERGH

"Oh for a book and a shady nook, either in door or out."

JOHN WILSON

LIBRARY DAYS

The public library became a haven to me on hot summer days when I was about 8 or 9 — I spent a good part of every summer luxuriating in the air-conditioned quiet there. The library was only a couple of blocks from my house so I walked there, barefoot & I remember how wonderful that cold, smooth floor felt on my hot little feet. I remember the way the library smelled — that good book smell & I remember walking home with my arms overflowing with romance, adventure, fantasy & inspiration. I adored fairy tales, The Red Book of Fairy Tales, The Yellow Book of Fairy Tales, every book of fairy tales. I loved books about big families like mine, The All of a Kind Family series was my favorite. When I was 15 I read Gone With the Wind & sobbed into my pillow at the end. I still have a copy of that sweet story Seventeenth Summer just for the feeling of that time of my life. Summer & books go hand-in-hand in my mind. I read on the porch swing, I read in a tree (I learned about reading in a tree from a book, of course). I read in my "secret place" (another book), I read at the beach, in the bathtub, in my bed, with my bologna sandwich, at the park & in the car. These days my favorite thing is to take my book & go out to lunch. I love finding things in old books so now I decorate the books I like best with a flower to dry between the pages; a leftover piece of artwork to use as a bookmark; or cartoons I think are funny — so someday in the future someone will find my little things & wonder about the person who put them there. Me! ♥

HOUSEWORK, WHEN DONE CORRECTLY,
CAN KILL YOU. ♡

How to go to a Tea Party

By Kitt Macy, Age 9

1. Wear a sutibul dress or skirt never pants or shorts.
2. Don't you ever go on Tuesdays or Friday the 13th.
3. Sip slowly, don't slurp.
4. Be jolly, laugh and eat at least 1 cookie.
5. Make an instring conversation.
6. Thank the host or hostist.
7. Give them at least 1 $.
8. After 5 times in a row the 6th time give a preasent.
9. Go again at least once.
10. Don't go and get things the host will bring it to you.
11. Have a great time!

" In the dell in our garden
My dolls and I take tea,
And days when I have raisins
The catbirds dine with me "

Elisabeth Merrill

♪♪ A country dance was being held in a garden...

GLUE IVY LEAVES
TO
EDGE OF
BUFFET TABLECLOTH

THE SUMMER TABLE

FLOAT PETALS OF SCENTED (ROSE) GERANIUM, FRUITS & BERRIES IN A GLASS OF CHAMPAGNE.

APPLE BASKETS, OLD COPPER KETTLES, LARGE WASH PANS, FUNNY PLASTIC POOL FLOATS— ALL MAKE GOOD "ICE CHESTS" FOR LARGE PARTIES.

SCATTER SUMMER SALADS LIBERALLY WITH FLOWERS & PETALS—PANSIES, NASTURTIUMS, VIOLETS, ROSE PETALS...

A GARDENIA CORSAGE— FOR MIDSUMMER EVE OR SATURDAY NIGHT MOVIE DATE.

FREEZE BORAGE FLOWERS IN ICE CUBES FOR LEMONADE OR TEA.

NAPKINS TIED WITH RIBBONS.

DAD

TINY CACTUS FOR PLACECARD HOLDERS.

PRESS A TINY FLOWER INTO A BUTTER PAT.

FLOWERS IN SAND FOR EACH PLACESETTING.

CHILDREN'S BEACH PAILS MAKE GREAT ICE BUCKETS.

VOTIVE CANDLE IN A SEASHELL.

DELICATE JAPANESE LANTERNS TO LIGHT THE GARDEN.
(SEE PG. 51)

SERVE SALADS, SAUCES & DIPS IN LARGE SEASHELLS

The perfect summer napkin ring is easy to make. Cut a 2 or 3 ft. runner of English ivy & strip the leaves from the bottom half. Wrap the leafy end around your hand & then weave the stripped end in & out & around — tuck in the end. Voilà! You can make these with any thin vine, such as a grapevine, & weave in tiny leaves later.

SOMETHING FISHY

My girlfriend hates fish & won't eat it because "It tastes fishy!" Fresh fish doesn't taste at <u>all</u> fishy — it's sweet & light & delicate. The problem is that really fresh fish is hard to find in some parts of the country. Well, WE get wonderful fish on Martha's Vineyard, so if you want the freshest, tastiest, cleanest swordfish, lobsters, monkfish, bay scallops (the tiny ones!), bluefish, clams, oysters, cod — & much more — you can call Louie at The Net Result here on the island & he'll ship your order overnight — guaranteed to be fresh. Call 1-800-394-6071.

El Rancho Margot's

SANTA FE SEAFOOD

350° Serves 8-10

Dinner for 8 all in one dish; cheesy corn polenta on the bottom, a layer of light white fish in the middle, covered in spicy carmelized onions — and you can make it ahead. ♥

Onions

¼ c. olive oil	1 c. "diced hot cherry peppers" (in
6 med.~large yellow onions	the pickle dept. at your mkt.)
2 tbsp. packed brown sugar	⅓ c. corn grits

Polenta

4 c. milk	¼ c. butter
1 tsp. salt	2 ~14oz. cans chopped green chilies, drained
2 c. corn grits	8 oz. sharp cheddar cheese, grated

3 lbs. fresh firm white fish: bass, cod, halibut, swordfish.

Heat oil over med. heat. Peel the onions, halve them & thinly slice. (Breathe through your mouth! Not your nose!) Cook slowly, stirring often — after 45 min. turn up the heat, evaporate liquid, lightly brown the onions; stir in sugar & peppers & continue cooking till most of the liquid is gone. Stir in corn grits. (While onions cook, make polenta.)

In med. saucepan bring milk & salt to almost boiling — over med. heat gradually whisk in grits — continue whisking till thick. Stir in butter, chilies & cheese. Spread evenly in a 9" x 13" x 2" baking dish. Preheat oven to 350°. Rinse & dry fish & layer it on top of the polenta. Spread onion mixture over fish evenly. Bake 45 min. Serve. ♥

♩ "SUMMER'S HERE AND THE TIME IS RIGHT FOR DANCING IN THE STREET." ♩

ZZZIPITY AY

SNOOZZIN'

ZZZIPITY DOO DAH

HAPPY DAYZZ ARE HERE AGAIN

I'M BIZZZY

BZZZZ

I LOVE SUMMERZZZ

STONEWALL BEACH
CRAB CAKES

Makes 16 3" cakes
Serves 8

I love them hot from the oven served on top of mixed greens with a few roasted vegetables & a little dressing or lemon juice. ♥

2 egg whites
2/3 c. mayonnaise
2 Tbsp. Dijon mustard
2 tsp. Worcestershire sauce
2 tsp. lemon juice
1/4 c. minced parsley
1/2 c. mixture of minced green onion
   & fresh chives (or green onion only)
1 1/4 tsp. cayenne
3/4 tsp. salt
2 lbs. lump crab meat, drained
1 1/2 c. fresh bread crumbs
lemon wedges

Mix together first 9 ingredients. Add the crab meat (make sure there's no shell in it) & 1/2 c. fresh bread crumbs. Mix carefully, not to break up the crab, until just combined. Form mixture into 16 3" cakes, coat each with bread crumbs & refrigerate them (on a plate) for an hour or more. ♥ To cook: Put the cakes on an oiled cookie sheet & broil them about 4" from heat for 4 min. on each side, till they're golden. Serve with lemon wedges. ♥

"WOE TO THE COOK WHOSE SAUCE HAS NO STING." ♥ CHAUCER

SPICE RUBBED FISH
WITH FRESH PEACH SALAD

Serves 4-6

This spicy fish can be grilled on the barbecue or cooked on one of those wonderful little stove-top grills — the cold peaches are a perfect cooler next to the fish. ♥

2 tbsp. paprika
4 tsp. lemon zest (use zester - easy!)
2 tsp. minced fresh ginger, patted with paper towel to remove excess moisture
2 tsp. finely minced parsley
2 tsp. black pepper
2 tsp. sesame seed
1 tsp. dill seed
1 tsp. cayenne
1 tsp. salt
½ tsp. mace
2 lb. thick fish fillets, halibut, swordfish, cod, tuna
olive oil

HANDY-DANDY LEMON ZESTER

Mix together first 10 ingred. Rinse & dry fish, brush with a little olive oil. Dredge fish lightly in spices, brushing off extra. Cook on oiled grill, turning once, over med. heat till opaque. (Always best to oil grill while cool.)

PEACH SALAD

COMBINE

2 lg. fresh peaches, pitted & diced   1 tbsp. chopped fresh mint
2 plums, seeded & diced   1 tbsp. chopped cilantro
¼ c. minced chives (or red onion)   1 tbsp. orange juice

SERVE COLD

CALAMARI SALAD

Serves 6

A rose by any other name would smell as sweet & squid by any other name would (& does) taste delicious! Serve it with cucumber sandwiches ♥

2 lb. calamari (squid), cleaned
¼ c. minced red pepper
¼ c. minced celery
½ c. olive oil
½ c. fresh lime juice
2 tbsp. orange marmalade
1 tbsp. minced lime zest
2 tbsp. chopped fresh cilantro (or parsley)
¼ tsp. Tabasco
1 tsp. salt
freshly ground pepper to taste

Slice calamari & tentacles into ¼" rings. Plunge into rapidly boiling water for 30 seconds (they become tough if overcooked). Drain, refresh in cold water. Put them in a bowl with red pepper & celery. Combine all other ingred. & pour over calamari. Chill well. ♥

"Dandelion wine. The words were summer on the tongue."
♥ Ray Bradbury

BARBECUED CHICKEN

Precook the chicken early in the day before it gets too hot & just pop it on the grill to finish it off with one of these delicious sauces come dinnertime. ♥

Chicken: 4 lbs. chicken serves 4-6. 2 c. sauce will do 4 lbs. chicken. Preheat oven to 350°. Remove skin from chicken pieces (under the faucet makes it easier) & reserve. Put the chicken into a deep casserole or dutch oven; lay the skin over the chicken & bake, uncovered, 45 min. Remove from oven & discard skin. Drain chicken, put it on a cookie sheet & brush liberally with sauce. Cook on grill about 5 min. each side, till sauce begins to blacken, basting with more sauce. (Also try Kitchen Sink BBQ Sauce, p. 90.) ♥

BOURBON CHICKEN
Makes 2 c.

1 c. apricot jam
1/2 c. bourbon
1/2 c. soy sauce
2 cloves garlic, minced

Slowly whisk bourbon & soy sauce into jam. Stir in garlic.

CAJUN CHICKEN
Makes 2 c.

1 c. olive oil
1/4 c. lemon juice
1/4 c. parsley
1/4 c. Cajun seasoning (Tony Chacheres' is very good.)
2 tbsp. brown sugar
2 tbsp. soy sauce
1/4 tsp. cayenne pepper

Whisk all ingredients together. ♥

LEMON CHICKEN
Makes 2 c.

1 stick butter, melted
juice of 2 lemons
1 bottle of beer (12 oz.)
salt & pepper

Mix all ingredients together. ♥

BARBECUED PORK RIBS

My sister Paula is the undisputed Queen of Barbecue in our family — her Kitchen Sink BBQ Sauce has everything in it & is ambrosia. If you are in a hurry, try the Pickapeppa Sauce, or for crusty Santa Maria-style ribs try the spicy rub on p. 96 ~ yum!

RIBS: 4 lbs. pork ribs serves 4. 2 c. sauce will do 4 lbs. ribs.

Preheat oven to 275°. Put rib slabs in roasting pan, uncovered, unsauced, just plain, for 2 hours. Heat up grill. Put as much sauce as you can on ribs, cook on both sides, basting with more sauce, till tinged with black — don't burn; remember, ribs are already cooked. Use tongs to turn meats. ♥

KITCHEN SINK BBQ SAUCE

Makes 2½ c.

2 Tbsp. olive oil
1 med. onion, chopped
1 clove garlic, minced
1 14 oz. bottle catsup
¼ c. Worcestershire sauce
¼ c. soy sauce
¼ c. beer

2 Tbsp. maple syrup
2 Tbsp. cider vinegar
½ tsp. dry mustard
¼ tsp. salt
¼ tsp. cayenne pepper
¼ tsp. Tabasco sauce

In a saucepan sauté onion & garlic in oil till limp. Add all remaining ingred. Stir, bring to boil & simmer 15 min. Remove from heat. This sauce improves with age. Keep in fridge.

PICKAPEPPA BBQ SAUCE

Makes 2 c.

Mix together:
1 - 8 oz. can crushed pineapple, drained
¾ c. Pickapeppa sauce

1 c. catsup
¼ tsp. cayenne

90

GRILLED SWORDFISH WITH PINEAPPLE SALSA & SWEET POTATO FRIES

Serves 4

Make **SALSA** 2 or 3 hours ahead so flavors can join forces. ♥

2 c. chopped fresh pineapple	1 clove garlic, pressed
1/2 c. minced red pepper	1/4 tsp. crushed red pepper
1/2 c. minced red onion	1/4 tsp. grated fresh ginger
1/4 c. finely chopped fresh mint	2 Tbsp. frozen o.j. concentrate
1/4 c. finely chopped cilantro	2 Tbsp. fresh lime juice

Chop everything carefully so you have a nice crisp consistency ~ mix it all together & put it into the refrigerator to chill. ♥

You need 2 lbs. **SWEET POTATOES** for 4 people ~ they shrink a bit. Preheat oven to 475°. Cut potatoes into 1/4" rounds (thin!). Pile them on a cookie sheet, drizzle with a tiny bit of olive oil ~ toss to coat, grind over fresh pepper, lay them in one layer. Roast 15 min., turn them with tongs, bake another 15 min. till edges start to turn dark brown.

You need 2 lbs. fresh **SWORDFISH**, about 1" thick. Also: 1/4 c. olive oil, 1 Tbsp. lime juice, 1 Tbsp. fresh rosemary and about 4 c. mixed greens (opt.). When you turn the potatoes over, that's the time to put the fish on the barbecue ~ baste it with mixture of olive oil, lime juice & rosemary. Cook until just done, about 7 min. each side.

TO SERVE: Put a handful of mixed greens on each plate ~ lay a piece of fish on top, put a big scoop of juicy salsa on top of fish & arrange potatoes, overlapping, on each side of fish. Serve. ♥

SALADE NIÇOISE

This is a special-occasion dish — a plateful of little treats, very make ahead, takes a little time but it's a flavor extravaganza & everyone will love you. 💜

Anchovy Mustard Dressing, p. 77.

2 c. greens per person, as many young tender varieties as possible, washed, dried, & gently torn.

Roasted Green Beans, p. 74 — you can tie them into little bundles with a piece of chive if you like.

Tomatoes. they should be the fresh garden variety, vine-ripened. Chop them small, put them in a bowl with a splash of red wine, a drizzle of olive oil, some slivered fresh basil, salt & freshly ground pepper to taste.

Rosemary Potatoes, p. 74.

Parsley Salad, p. 71.

Fresh Artichoke Hearts: very deliciously decadent. Steam one whole artichoke per person; cool completely. Recklessly with abandon tear off & remove all leaves; get right to the heart. (Put leaves in the compost). Clean the hearts, put them on a plate, sprinkle with lemon juice. In another bowl,

mix together mayonnaise, lots of Parmesan cheese, a
   squeeze of fresh lemon & a bit of minced tarragon. Put
   a spoonful in the hollow of each heart. Chill.
Roasted Red Peppers, p. 75.
Hard-Boiled Eggs: one per person, very best served fresh
   & warm & a little underdone. Halve them; S & p.
Olives: either Niçoise or calamata, about 5 each.
Grilled Portobello Mushrooms: p. 57.   Cook at the same
   time you do the fish, about 3 slices per person.
Grilled Tuna, about 1/3 lb. per person. Tuna makes it
   classic but you can also use swordfish or salmon.
      Also very good with Crab Cakes, p. 86-or Cajun Shrimp, p. 95.
Fresh Nasturtiums, one per person.
Lemon Wedges: quarter them & tie them into a   little
   piece of cheesecloth with a piece of string, one per person.

Make dressing. Arrange about 2 c. fresh greens on each
plate & sprinkle over a spoonful of dressing for each.
Around the edge of each plate, keeping color in mind, put
a small amt. of each ingredient, keeping them separate: a
bundle of green beans, a little pile of tomatoes, a small
serving of potatoes, etc., up to the olives (save a space for mushrooms). When ready to serve, light an oiled barbecue, grill
the fish & mushrooms. Put a piece of hot grilled fish in
the center of each salad, put sliced mushrooms on the side &
top everything with a fresh nasturtium. Serve with lemon
wedges; pass dressing separately. ♥

"God has given us our memories
that we might have roses in December."
♥ J. M. Barrie

POTATO FISH CAKES
with Whole-Grain Mustard Sauce

Makes 6 4" cakes

Great served as a main dish with a green salad & some grilled mushrooms. Also good cooked in an iron pan over an open fire — take them camping. ♥

2 lbs. red potatoes
2 ½ tbsp. butter
⅓ c. chopped parsley
½ tsp. salt
lots of freshly ground pepper
⅓ lb. smoked bluefish, trout, or mullet

⅓ c. hot milk
flour for dredging
oil for frying
½ c. whole-grain mustard
½ c. sour cream

Halve the potatoes & cook them (skins on) in boiling salted water until tender. Drain & mash (with skins) coarsely; add butter, parsley, salt & pepper & stir well. Remove fish skin & chop smoked fish; add to dish. Pour hot milk over all, mix well. Form this chunky mixture into 4" cakes. Dredge lightly in flour & fry in vegetable oil till browned. Mix together the mustard & sour cream, & serve a spoonful alongside fish cakes. ♥

"MANNERS ARE A SENSITIVE AWARENESS OF THE FEELINGS OF OTHERS. IF YOU HAVE THAT AWARENESS, YOU HAVE GOOD MANNERS, NO MATTER WHAT FORK YOU USE."

Emily Post ♥

Joke du jour: "We live in New England where you love your husband so much you almost tell him." ♡

BEACH STREET
CAJUN SHRIMP
450° Serves 4

Here's one way to show your husband you love him — cook him up a plate of Cajun Shrimp. :)

½ c. olive oil	2 Tbsp. minced parsley
1 clove garlic, whole	1 Tbsp. brown sugar
2 Tbsp. Cajun seasoning	1 Tbsp. soy sauce
2 Tbsp. lemon juice	16 extra-large shrimp

Combine first 7 ingredients in a 9 x 13 baking dish. Shell & devein the shrimp, pat dry & toss in marinade to coat. Refrigerate 1-12 hrs. Preheat oven to 450°. Remove garlic clove. Bake for 7-10 min., stirring occasionally — be sure not to overcook. ♡ You can also grill them on skewers. Delicious served with Lemon Linguini (p. 70). ♡

"A dinner invitation, once accepted, is a sacred obligation. If you die before the dinner takes place, your executor must attend."
♡ Ward McAllister

95

GRILLED STEAKS
SANTA MARIA STYLE

Serves 4 to 8

Thick, juicy steaks from the grill with a spicy crust — if you like crusty meat, try this on ribs or hamburgers, too. ♥

4 rib-eye steaks, 1½"–2" thick
2 Tbsp. freshly ground
   black pepper
2 Tbsp. salt
2 Tbsp. brown sugar

2 Tbsp. white sugar
2 Tbsp. chili powder
2 Tbsp. cumin
1 Tbsp. cayenne
¼ c. paprika

Oven-broil or pan-broil steaks ahead of time, until just rare. Mix together all remaining ingredients. Light grill. When you are ready to eat, brush steaks with olive oil & dredge them in spices. Cook them on the grill, turning once, till done to your liking. Watch closely, don't burn. ♥

"I expand and live in the warm day like corn and melons."
♡ Ralph Waldo Emerson

OLD-FASHIONED PICNIC
MENU

Bread & Butter Pickles ♥ Pitted Black Olives ♥ Celery Stuffed with Cream Cheese, Sprinkled with Paprika ♥ Salted Radishes & Green Onions ♥ Stuffed Eggs ♥ Fried Chicken ♥ Potato Salad ♥ Bean Salad ♥ Waldorf Salad ♥ Watermelon Slices ♥ Strawberry Shortcake ♥ Blueberry Pie ♥ Coconut Layer Cake ♥ Iced Tea with Lemon, Sugar & Mint ♥ Homemade Lemonade

BRING ALONG A Jar of Water for Just-Picked Wildflowers ♥

97

Fragile

WILDFLOWER

I found it on
my walk this
morning — out
in the woods,
all by itself.

She seeds are
slow to spread so
we never pick them —
enjoy them where
they sit.

Lady's Slipper
(unpredictable)

means "Capricious (fickle or
Beauty)" in flower language.

LADY'S SLIPPER

SPOTTED IN THE WOODS
June 19TH

Martha's Vineyard

98

HERB VINEGAR

NASTURTIUMS, SEEDS OR SPICES WHOLE ZEST, LIME OR LEMON PEPPERS, CHILI HOT CLOVES, GARLIC TRY

OIL BOTTLES, WATER BOTTLES, SALAD

RECYCLE WINE BOTTLES, OLIVE

DRESSING & MAPLE SYRUP.

nice bottles & corks

RED WINE, CIDER, OR WHITE

USE ANY KIND, TRY

WINE VINEGAR.

one quart vinegar

THYME OR SAGE FOR MEAT MAR-

SLIGHTLY BRUISE HERB · USE

INADE. ❧ DILL FOR FISH.

one cup fresh herb

steep it 2 or 3 days

MAKE SURE ALL

HERBS ARE SUBMERGED.

in a sunny window

ARE AT THE

CORKS OF ALL SIZES

HARDWARE STORE.

strain, if you like

PLACE. ❧ LABEL & TIE WITH RIBBON

STORE IN A COOL DARK

FOR A NICE HOMEMADE GIFT.

Chive Vinegar

add fresh herb sprig

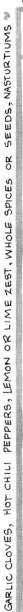

CAMPING

Ah...camping. I'm a veteran of the camping wars. Camping was my parents' idea of the perfect vacation for them & their 8 children; we went every summer. We loved it, but I have a hard time understanding why they did! We had to take everything with us: tents, sleeping bags, high chair, stroller, playpen, diapers for 2 weeks, food for 2 weeks, clothes, pots & pans. We kids were perched on top of all this, packed in between pillows & cereal boxes in the big old station wagon with the wood on the sides.

WE'RE OFF TO SEE THE WIZARD...

ARE WE THERE YET?

USA

Off we'd go ~ 8 hours on the road to Sequoia National Park (8hrs! 8 kids!). We knew all the car songs & car games, but every year we would hit those hair-pin turns toward the end of the trip & all ~ all of us threw up ~ every year ~ out all the windows. Up & back. Just part of the trip ~ perfectly normal.

We have photographs of us having a wonderful time ~ pitching the tent, around the campfire, in our sleeping bags, luring squirrels, doing dishes, dangling our legs over high cliffs, catching rattle snakes (4 brothers I have), swimming & fishing; us with park rangers, us climbing rocks & us standing in groups for family pictures. We still have the ice chest bearing the dents & scars of the bear claw that was after our bacon, & the scary photograph of him in the trees standing on his hind legs. Our tent was 9' × 15' & divided into 3 rooms ~ one for the boys, one for the girls & one for Mom & Dad. Bedtime, the whole family would be tucked into their sleeping bags ~ talking, talking in the dark, safe inside the tent, till we fell asleep. Parents' quiet voices in the night are a very reassuring thing to kids in tents ♥.

In the morning my dad would get up first & make a big fire, then pretty soon Mom would start frying bacon ~ that outdoor morning smell of bacon & wood smoke still sends me to the moon ~ nothing tastes better than food in the "wild." GO CAMPING!

(TAKE ME!)

(JUST PLEASE DON'T MAKE ME SIT IN THE "WAY BACK.")

"Once in a young lifetime one should be allowed to have as much sweetness as one can possibly want & hold." 💜 Judith Olney

FRUITS
Pies
Pudding
CAKE
ICES
ice cream
Drinks

WATERMELON

Before you go off to the beach or lake, put a watermelon in the fridge to chill. Ice-cold watermelon tastes heavenly when you've just come home from the beach & everybody is sandy & hot & sticky in their bathing suits in the yard. (The sprinkler is especially good then, too.)

Sing a Song of Watermelon, Mark Twain

"I know how a prize watermelon looks when it is sunning its fat rotundity among pumpkin vines; I know how inviting it looks when it is cooling itself in a tub of water under the bed, waiting; I know how a boy looks behind a yard-long slice of that melon, and I know how he feels; for I have been there."

"WHEN ONE HAS TASTED WATERMELON HE KNOWS WHAT THE ANGELS EAT."
Mark Twain

As kids, we weren't allowed to eat watermelon anywhere but curbside or in somebody else's yard — anyplace but our yard! There were so many of us, my dad was finding it difficult to keep up with the number of watermelon plants popping up all over — they were everywhere ♥ We always wished ice cream had seeds!

HOMEMADE
Fresh Strawberry Ice Cream
Makes 3 pints

You need ripe, juicy, in-season strawberries — also an ice cream maker. The ones today are great because you can actually bring them to the table, a few stirs & voilà, ice cream! ♥

2 c. whole milk
2 c. heavy cream
1¼ c. sugar
1½ c. puréed fresh, ripe strawberries

Lick ~ Lick ~ Lick

Bring milk & cream just to boiling point. Remove from heat, add ¾ c. of sugar, stir to dissolve. Cool. 🍓🍓 Purée the strawberries in a food processor until liquid. Add the rest of the sugar (½ c.) to purée & stir. Blend milk mixture with the purée, taste for sweetness & freeze in ice cream maker. Serve. ♥ Keep any left-over mixture & make more tomorrow!

"I value my garden more for being full of blackbirds 🕊 than of cherries 🍒, and very frankly give them fruit for their songs."

♥ Joseph Addison

Crunchy Granola Ice Cream Squares with Caramel Sauce

9 Squares

3½ c. really good granola (p.121)
(say no thankyou to diet granola)
½ c. Hershey's chocolate syrup

1 qt. vanilla ice cream, softened
Caramel Sauce (below)

Spread 2c. granola evenly in the bottom of a 9"x9" pan. Drizzle chocolate sauce over the granola & spread on the softened ice cream as evenly as possible. Sprinkle remaining 1½ c. granola over ice cream & press down gently & make it level. Freeze till ready to serve. Cut into squares & serve with either cold or heated Caramel Sauce. ♥

Caramel Sauce

1 c. sugar
3 Hbsp. water   1 c. heavy cream

Heat sugar & water together in non-aluminum pan. Bring to simmer & cook without stirring until amber in color. Heat cream in another pan. When sugar is amber, slowly pour in hot cream, whisking constantly until well blended. Good hot or cold. ♥

"KNOW YOU WHAT IT IS TO BE A CHILD? IT IS TO BE VERY DIFFERENT FROM THE MAN OF TODAY. IT IS TO HAVE A SPIRIT YET STREAMING FROM THE WATERS OF BAPTISM; IT IS TO BELIEVE IN LOVE, TO BELIEVE IN LOVELINESS, TO BELIEVE IN BELIEF; IT IS TO BE SO LITTLE THAT THE ELVES CAN REACH TO WHISPER IN YOUR EAR..." ♥ FRANCIS THOMPSON

LAVENDER TEA COOKIES

These "biscuits," as my English pen pal Rachel calls them, spread like crazy while baking — but the lavender flavor is so exotic — — you can almost taste breath of bees in them (no, they don't taste like soap!). ♡ Serve them with creamy vanilla ice cream. ♡

350° Makes 30
Line cookie sheet with parchment paper
1 c. unsalted butter
2/3 c. minus 1 Tbsp. superfine sugar
1 egg, beaten
1¼ c. minus 1 Tbsp. self-rising flour
1 Tbsp. fresh lavender flowers

Preheat oven to 350°. Cream butter & sugar, add egg & beat well. Stir in flour & flowers. Drop teaspoonsful on parchment, spacing widely to allow for spread. Bake 15-20 min. until pale golden & edges tinge brown. They will be soft until cooled on waxed paper. Store in airtight tin. ♡

"DON'T HURRY, DON'T WORRY. YOU'RE ONLY HERE FOR A SHORT VISIT. SO BE SURE TO STOP AND SMELL THE FLOWERS."
♡ Walter C. Hagen

ICED RED WINE SNOW

Serves 8

Snow cones for grown-ups. The better the wine, the better this will taste. Very light & positively delicious.

1 c. water
3/4 c. sugar
2 c. good red wine, a
   Cabernet or Pinot Noir

about 4" cinnamon sticks
3/4 c. fresh lemon juice
1½ c. cranberry juice

In a saucepan, stir water, sugar, wine & cinnamon sticks together, bring to a boil, reduce heat & simmer 10 min. Remove from heat & stir in juices; refrigerate until cold. Pour in a 9" x 9" pan & put it in the freezer. Give it a stir every ½ hr. or so with a fork to break up crystals, until frozen — about 3 hrs. Before serving let it sit out for a few minutes until slightly soft — beat with a whisk till fluffy & scoop into bowls or goblets. ♥

"I bought a dress, a romantic dress, a purely summer party dress: white, splashed with large pink dots, a floppy full skirt and bared shoulders. A dress for a summer tan, a summer dance."

Alice Adams

Blueberry Bread Pudding

325° Serves 10-12

Serve hot with hot Blueberry Sauce & vanilla ice cream, or serve cold with cold Blueberry Sauce & whipped cream. Great for a brunch, too. ♥

1 lg. loaf day~old French bread, in 3/4" cubes, about 12 c.
3 eggs
2 c. milk
3 tbsp. vanilla
1 c. sugar
3/4 tsp. cinnamon

3/4 tsp. nutmeg
2 c. blueberries
2 c. fresh peaches pitted & peeled
3/4 c. butter, cut into bits
3 tbsp. cinnamon
2 tsp. nutmeg

Preheat oven to 325°. Butter a 9"x13" baking dish. Put cut-up bread into a large colander — pour about 4 c. hot tap water over bread evenly. Leave for 5 min. — press out excess water & set aside. Plunge peaches into boiling water for about 12 seconds, peel & chop into 1" pieces. In a large bowl, whisk together eggs, milk, vanilla, sugar & spices. Gently fold in bread, berries & peaches. Pour into baking dish. Drop butter bits evenly over the top. Mix together cinnamon & nutmeg & sprinkle evenly over pudding. Bake 1 hr. & 20 min. Serve hot or cold. ♥

Blueberry Sauce

2 c. good red wine
3 c. blueberries
6" of cinnamon stick

½ c. sugar
2 tbsp. arrowroot

Bring wine, blueberries, cinnamon sticks & sugar to the boil; cover & simmer 10 min. Gradually whisk in arrowroot, stir till thickened. Remove cinnamon sticks before serving. ♥

COCONUT
LAYER CAKE
WITH LEMON FILLING

This is an old-fashioned, big tall coconut cake, the perfect summer cake, three soft layers with a heavenly lemon filling, frosted with a wonderful marshmallow-like frosting & covered in coconut.

Lemon Filling

Juice & grated rind of 2 lemons
1 c. sugar
2 eggs, beaten
2 Tbsp. butter, melted

When grating rind take special care not to get the bitter white part. Put all ingred. in double boiler, stir over simmering water till thickened ~15-20 min. Chill.

Cake

Makes 3 8" layers

6 Tbsp. butter, room temp.
1½ c. sugar
3 eggs, separated
2¼ c. flour, sifted

3 tsp. baking powder
¼ tsp. salt
3/4 c. milk
1 tsp. vanilla

Preheat oven to 350°. Cream butter & sugar. Add egg yolks & beat until thick & lemon-colored. With a fork, mix together dry ingred. & add them to egg mixture alternately with the milk; stir in vanilla. Fold in stiffly beaten egg whites. Divide batter between 3 buttered 8" cake pans & bake at 350° for 20 min. Cool completely & remove from pans. Before frosting cut off rough edges of cake with sharp scissors.

A perfect birthday cake

Continued ⟶

WONDERFUL
MARSHMALLOW-LIKE
Frosting

The classic boiled frosting, pure white, shiny & fluffy. You'll need a candy thermometer. ♥

1/3 c. water	pinch of salt
1 c. sugar	2 egg whites
1/8 tsp. cream of tartar	1 tsp. vanilla
sweetened coconut	

Stir the water, sugar, cream of tartar & salt together in a small heavy-bottomed pan. Hook a candy thermometer to the edge of the pan & boil without stirring until mixture reaches 240°F. Meanwhile, beat egg whites until stiff. Pour the 240° syrup over the whites in a thin stream, beating constantly until thick & glossy. Stir in vanilla. Frost the cake ~ pat & sprinkle coconut onto sides & over the top. ❀

To Assemble

Put the chilled filling between cooled layers ~ try not to let too much of it get out the sides. Frost the cake then sprinkle on coconut thickly, gently pressing it into the sides. During this process the cake may try to slip & slide, but just slide it back straight. I decorate the cake with 3 raspberries in the center with 3 lemon balm leaves 🍃, or with a tiny cluster of currant berries, or around the 🍃 outside edge with blueberries; especially charming sprinkled with violets. ♥

"Women sit or move to and fro, some
old, some young. The young are
beautiful ~ but the old are more
beautiful than the young."
Walt Whitman ♥

109

FRUIT DESSERTS

Sliced Peaches & Cream
Briefly dip whole ripe peaches into boiling water, peel with a sharp knife & cut into slices. Sprinkle with sugar & chill at least one hour. Serve with or without a wee soupçon of heavy cream.

Cantaloupe & Ice Cream
Cut a cantaloupe in half, scrape out seeds & fill cavity with a scoop of vanilla ice cream. Great for a special brunch.

Lemon Ice
Hollow out whole lemons & fill them with Lemon Ice & freeze them. To serve: pile them in a pyramid & tuck in mint sprigs. Recipe: 3½ c. water 1¼ c. sugar ¾ c. fresh lemon juice 2 tbsp. lemon zest. Boil water, stir in sugar until dissolved, add lemon juice & zest & freeze in a bowl. Remove from freezer, beat till fluffy, fill lemons & refreeze till ready to serve.

Watermelon Surprise
Remove visible seeds from a slice of watermelon, spread with sour cream & sprinkle over brown sugar. (The surprise happens when your tastebuds explode!)

Chocolate-Dipped Strawberries
Dip whole perfect ripe strawberries into melted bitter-sweet chocolate. Set on waxed paper to dry.

Red, White & Blueberry Sundaes
Strawberry ice cream drizzled with blueberry sauce topped with whipped cream & a big fresh strawberry. Blueberry Sauce next page

Blueberry Sauce
Delicious over ice cream.
12 oz. fresh or frozen wild blueberries, 1/3 c. water, 1/3 c. sugar, & 1 tsp. grated lemon rind. Place all ingredients in a non-aluminum saucepan & bring to a boil. Simmer gently for 10 min. Serve hot or cold.

Fruit Fondue with Orange Chocolate Sauce
Skewer fresh strawberries, pineapple, bananas, pears, apples & pieces of angel food cake & dip them into this heated chocolate sauce: 12 oz. semi-sweet chocolate, 2/3 c. heavy cream & 2 tbsp. orange liqueur. Heat chocolate & cream, stirring over low heat till chocolate melts. Stir in liqueur. Keep warm over very low heat.

Watermelon Whale
Cut a whole watermelon into the shape of a whale & hollow it out. *VIEW FROM THE TOP* Fill the cavity with fresh fruit, strawberries, cantaloupe (use a melon baller), raspberries, red grapes, bananas, & watermelon. Darling at a pot luck barbecue or picnic.

Baked Bananas with Ice Cream
Put one ripe banana per person on a cookie sheet (in its skin). Bake at 350° until it turns completely black, about 20 min. Slit open & moosh up, same as you would with a baked potato. Serve with a scoop of vanilla ice cream & a sprinkle of fresh ground coffee.

Almost Fruit ~ for the kids
Hollow out halved oranges & fill with Jell-O. Serve with a dot of whipped cream. This makes 10 halves: make a 6 oz. pkg. of Jell-O according to instructions except use only 1½ c. boiling water.

CHERRY ORANGES!

DESSERT!   DESSERT!   DESSERT!

PINEAPPLE UPSIDE-DOWN CAKE
WITH VANILLA SAUCE

350° Serves 8

Try not to drink the sauce; it's perfect with this old-fashioned picnic cake. ♥

3 Tbsp. butter
3/4 c. brown sugar
1 lb. can pineapple rings
walnut halves
3 eggs
1 c. sugar

1/2 c. juice drained from pineapple
1 1/2 tsp. vanilla
1 1/2 c. sifted flour
1/2 tsp. baking powder
1/2 tsp. salt

Preheat oven to 350°. Melt 3 Tbsp. butter in a 9" oven-proof skillet, or any straight-sided pan ~ I use a spring-form. Sprinkle in brown sugar. Arrange pineapple slices (saving the juice) over the sugar ~ put walnuts in pineapple centers & around edges. Put pan into oven to warm (but don't cook). In a med. bowl beat eggs till fluffy; gradually beat in sugar. Add pineapple syrup & vanilla. Sift flour, baking powder & salt; add all at once & beat smooth. Pour over pineapple. Bake 50 min. Turn out onto cake plate. Looks great decorated with calendulas around the edge ~ marigolds too. Put a puddle of Vanilla Sauce on a plate ~ put a slice of cake right smack in the middle of it. Serve. ♥

VANILLA SAUCE

1" piece of vanilla bean
2 c. heavy cream

1/4 c. sugar

Slit vanilla bean in half & scrape pulp into a small saucepan. Stir in cream & bring to a boil. Add sugar, stir & let it cool. Chill well. ♥

PEACH  & PLUM CRISP

350° Serves 8-10

Thank goodness for good friends, otherwise who could feel comfortable serving a pie with a piece already missing? I only meant to taste the edge of topping & then the phone rang & I picked, nibbled, got a spoon & did the pie. I should call it "Bye Pie." WAVE BYE-BYE. ♥

Filling: 4 med. peaches, peeled & pitted
2½ lbs. plums, pitted
½ c. sugar

2 Tbsp. quick-cooking tapioca
1 tsp. fresh lemon juice
pinch of salt

Topping: ½ c. butter, softened
½ c. brown sugar
3/4 c. flour
3/4 c. oats

¼ c. chopped walnuts
2 tsp. lemon zest
½ tsp. cinnamon

Butter a 10 in. glass or pottery pie plate (2" deep). Peel peaches by dipping each briefly in boiling water. Cut them & plums into wedges. Mix together all ingred. for filling, put into pie plate. Let stand 1 hr.; stir occasionally. Preheat oven to 350°. Mix together topping ingred., spread evenly over fruit. Bake on center rack in oven; put a cookie sheet on lower rack to catch juices. Serve hot with ice cream or cold with whipped cream. ♥ (Good with phone too. ♥)

"Charm: the quality in others that makes us more satisfied with ourselves."
♥ Henri-Frédérik Amiel

GREEN APPLE & BLUEBERRY TART

400° Serves 6~8

This is a rustic country pie ~ it's free-form & easy to make.

½ lb. frozen puff pastry, thawed
  (available at grocery stores)
4 green apples, peeled, cored,
  cut into ¼" slices
1 c. fresh (or frozen) blueberries
2 Tbsp. fresh lemon juice

¼ c. brown sugar
2 Tbsp. white sugar
2 Tbsp. flour
¾ tsp. cinnamon
1 Tbsp. butter
powdered sugar

Preheat oven to 400°. Roll out pastry to a 14" circle on a lightly floured surface. Transfer to a large cookie sheet & chill. Put fruit in a large bowl & toss with lemon juice. Add sugars, flour & cinnamon, mix well. Evenly arrange fruit mixture in center of pastry, leaving a 2" border. Fold edge of pastry up & over apple mixture in overlapping folds to form sides of pie. (There should be a 4 to 5" opening in the middle — feel comfortable, nothing here is supposed to be perfect.) Brush folds with a little water at edges & pinch to seal. Cut butter into bits over fruit; sprinkle tart with a little granulated sugar & bake 40 min. If pastry gets too brown, cover tart with a piece of foil. Cool 10 min., slide onto serving plate. Sift over a bit of powdered sugar & serve. ♥

"One comes back to these old-fashioned roses as one does to music and old poetry. A garden needs old associations, old fragrances, as a home needs things that have been lived with." ♥ Marion Page

PROFITEROLES

375° Makes 12 puffs   Serves 6

1/4 c. butter
1/2 c. water
1/2 c. flour
2 eggs, room temp.

2 pts. vanilla ice cream, softened
Chocolate Sauce (below)
1 c. heavy cream, whipped with 1 tsp.
vanilla & sugar to taste

Preheat oven to 375°. Boil butter & water together in a small saucepan. Remove from heat; add flour all at once, beating rapidly till dough leaves side of pan & forms a ball. Cool 5 min. Add eggs, one at a time, beating hard till dough is smooth. Drop teaspoonsful (12) on ungreased cookie sheet 2" apart. Bake 16-20 min. till golden brown. Cool. Set ice cream out to soften. With serrated knife, carefully cut off top 3rd of each puff; remove wet dough inside. Fill with as much ice cream as you can & replace tops. Pile them into a bowl; keep them in freezer till ready to serve (a few hrs.). Make chocolate. When ready, whip cream, reheat chocolate till pourable. Cover frozen puffs with half the chocolate, then the cream. Serve; pass rest of chocolate separately. ♥

Chocolate Sauce: Makes 2 c.: 1 c. sweetened condensed milk; 10 oz. good bittersweet chocolate; 1/2 c + 1 Tbsp. hot water; 1/4 tsp. salt; 2 tsp. vanilla. Combine milk, chocolate, water & salt in heavy pan; stir over low heat till smooth & blended. Stir in vanilla. ♥

ICED
CAFFÈ LATTE

mmmm mmmm good. A little more
sophisticated for picnics, garden parties.

6 c. strong coffee
2 heaping tablespoons of sugar
1½-2c. mixed half & half
& whole milk

Measurements are approximate. Brew
a large pot of coffee, decaf or regular,
& add an extra measure of coffee.
Pour it into a large pitcher & add
other ingred. to taste. It should be
strong & milky & slightly sweet.
Refrigerate & serve over ice. ♥

Fresh
LEMON-LIMEADE

Makes 1½ quarts

¼ c. water
¼ c. sugar
zest from 1 lemon
zest from 1 lime
juice of 3 lemons
juice of 3 limes
5 c. cold water

In a small saucepan bring water to boil; add sugar & stir until dissolved. Remove from heat. Add zest (don't get the bitter white part) & the juice to the sugar water. To make a pitcherful, stir mixture into 5c. cold water & add ice. ⁓ Or, keep in fridge & make one or two glasses at a time whenever you want. A slice of lemon & a sprig of mint, lots of ice & a couple of straws make it a party! ♥

Country life has its conveniences," he would sometimes say. "You sit on the veranda and drink tea, while your ducks swim on the pond, there is a delicious smell everywhere... and the gooseberries are growing."
♥ Anton Chekhov

SKIP & GO NAKED

These are really delicious! And _pink_, like Double Bubble gum. All my friends have a "Skip & Go Naked" story & now you can too! (THAT IS, IF YOU _WANT_ ONE.) ♥

Makes 2 big drinks

2/3 c. cold beer
2/3 c. frozen pink lemonade concentrate
1/4 c. vodka
straws or stirrers

Fill blender container 1/2 way with ice. Pour in beer, lemonade & vodka, blend well & serve. ♡ I served delicate little sherry glassfuls to my girlfriends at lunch~ icy, pink perfection (just like us! ☺). ♥

"THE STANDARD OF PER-FECTION FOR VODKA (NO COLOR, NO TASTE, NO SMELL) ACCOUNTS PERFECTLY FOR THE DRINK'S RISING POPULARITY WITH THOSE WHO LIKE THEIR ALCOHOL IN CONJUNCTION WITH THE REASSURING TASTES OF INFANCY~ JELL-O, ORANGE JUICE, PINK LEMON-ADE. IT IS THE IDEAL INTOXICANT FOR THE DRINKER WHO WANTS NO REMINDER OF HOW HURT MOTHER WOULD BE IF SHE KNEW." AFTER A.J. LIEBLING

JELL-O SHOOTERS

Pass a plateful to party goers; they almost feel like sin, but it's only Jell-O made dangerous!

1 6 oz. pkg. Jell-O (red or blue)   1 1/3 c. vodka or rum
1 pkg. Knox gelatine (2 tsp.)   2/3 c. cold water

Add 2 c. boiling water to Jell-O & gelatine~ stir 2 min. Stir in vodka & cold water; pour into 9" x 9" pan. Chill until set. Cut into squares. (Shoot in moderation.) ♥

" WE ONCE HAD A LILY HERE THAT BORE
108 FLOWERS ON ONE STALK: IT WAS PHOTOGRAPHED
NATURALLY FOR ALL THE GARDENING PAPERS.
THE BEES CAME FROM MILES AND MILES, AND
THERE WERE THE MOST DISGRACEFUL
BACCHANALIAN SCENES: BEES HARDLY
ABLE TO FIND THEIR WAY HOME."

♥ Edith Sitwell

Have you ever had a Pimm's Cup? It's veddy, veddy English
& the perfect accompaniment to croquet. The bees knees,
actually, & quite brilliant ☺.

PIMM'S CUP

1 oz. (2 Tbsp.) gin	splash of orange juice
2 oz. (¼ c.) Pimm's	slice of orange or lemon
ginger ale	(or cucumber)

Put gin & Pimm's (get it at the liquor store) into a 14 oz. glass
(I have those French jelly glasses) — fill glass with
ice, add ginger ale almost to top, then a splash of o.j.
Finish off with a slice of fresh orange or lemon or, as
the English do, a bit of cucumber. ♥

Mornings, Sweet, Sweet, Sweet.

"At breakfast that morning (a
simple meal of marmalade spread lightly
over a honeycomb or two) he had suddenly
thought of a new song. It began like this:
♪ 'Sing Ho! for the life of a Bear,';"
Winnie-the-Pooh 💜

Kiwi Cup

This is a darling start for a summer
breakfast party — egg cups filled
with peeled & sliced kiwi fruit,
surrounded with Johnny-jump-ups. 💜

Summer Baked Apple

350° Serves 6

Yellow apple, fresh mint — a lovely way to start the day. 💜

6 Golden Delicious apples
3 Tbsp. brown sugar
3 Tbsp. chopped walnuts
1/4 c. soft butter
6 Tbsp. oats
3/4 tsp. cinnamon

3/4 tsp. nutmeg
1 Tbsp. lemon juice
1 c. apple juice
6 fresh mint sprigs
1 1/4 c. half & half

Preheat oven to 350°. Core each apple, careful not to break through
bottom — leave lots of room for filling. Mix together next 7 ingred.
Fill apples, place in baking dish, pour apple juice around &
bake 25 min. Set each in a small dish, pour over a little cream,
garnish with mint & serve. 💜

SARAH'S
GRANOLA

Makes approx. 2½ quarts

Homemade is best — delicious with yogurt & fresh, juicy fruit for breakfast; sprinkled over ice cream & chocolate sauce or eaten as a snack. Chock-full of vitamins!

1 lb. (5c.) oats
⅓ lb. (1c.) raw sunflower seeds
¼ c. raw sesame seeds
½ c. wheat germ
½ c. unsalted cashews, chopped
½ c. sliced almonds

¼ c. vegetable oil
½ c. honey
½ c. maple syrup
1½ c. unsweetened
   coconut "chips"
¾ c. raisins

All ingredients can be purchased at your health food store. Preheat oven to 400°. Combine the first 9 ingred. & spread on cookie sheets in one layer. Bake 20-25 min., stirring occasionally. Add coconut chips for last 5 min. The granola should be a golden, toasted color. Remove from oven & cool. Add raisins. Store in an airtight container. ♥ Great to take camping, on car or train trips.

"Health is the thing that makes
   you feel like now is the best time
      of the year." ♥ Franklin Pierce Adams

JULY 14, 1994

OH-OH— LOOK WHAT I FOUND ON
MY WALK
TODAY.
IT SIGNIFIES
YOU-KNOW-WHAT!

" WHEN THE DAYS BEGIN TO
SHORTEN, SOON AFTER SOLSTICE
ON JUNE 21, A TREE RECONSIDERS
ITS LEAVES."

A NATURAL HISTORY OF THE SENSES

FARE THEE WELL

Rain or shine, sleet or snow storm, we walk 3 miles out the same dirt road through the woods every morning. It's a wonderful vantage point to enjoy the changing seasons; we see the migration of birds, the changes in foliage; the light, tides, sunrises, the sea — as one season slowly but surely fades into another. Now summer is winding down & we see the proof of it when we walk out to the end where the pond opens into the sound — colors have already changed, the last of the fragrant beach roses is just gone, replaced by berry-red rose hips. But the most noticeable difference is with the little cottages — some have already been boarded up for the season — protected against ice & sea & salt till next year. The dogs are gone; the station wagons loaded to the gills with beach chairs, fishing poles & summer people totter past us on the road. The houses sit alone now, no towels flapping from the porches; flags are down, just the windswept beach grass yellow & gold. Altho' the days are still warm, there's the constant hum of crickets in the air & you can feel just the tiniest chill in the breeze off the sea. I'm going to miss the smell of those breakfasts-by-the-sea cooking every morning — coffee, bacon, eggs & toast wafting on the wind all summer long, but those that stay year 'round have begun to light their stoves & the smell of woodsmoke goes well with swirling leaves, honking geese & the sea (and me!). We stop to pick the last blueberry & Kiss Summer Goodbye. ♥

"And when the rain beats against my window Pane

THANK YOU TO LIT TLE, BROWN PEOP
LE WHO HAVE BEEN SO WONDERFUL TO M
E FROM THE VERY BEGINNING & ESPECIAL
LY MARY TONDORF-DICK. THANK YOU TO ED
ITE KROLL WHO IS ALWAYS ON MY SIDE AND
THANK YOU TO MY FAMILY & FRIEND
S FOR LOVING ME & BEING MY FRIE
NDS AND LAST BUT NOT LEAST I
WANT TO THANK MY JOSEPH
B HALL, GUARDIAN AN
GEL EXTRAORDINA
IRE & ♥ TOM
OM & DA
D

I'll think of summer days again & dream of you."

Chad & Jeremy

Send your name & address to me (Susan Branch) at P.O. Box 2463B, Vineyard Haven, MA 02568 & I'll put you on my mailing list! ♥

Index

"Thank heavens, the sun has gone in, & I don't have to go out & enjoy it."
♥ Logan Pearsall Smith